M000158148

VINDICIAE CONTRA TYRANNOS: A DEFENSE OF LIBERTY AGAINST TYRANTS

VINDICIAE CONTRA TYRANNOS: A DEFENSE OF LIBERTY AGAINST TYRANTS

A TREATISE WRITTEN BY
STEPHEN JUNIUS BRUTUS

Translated by William Walker
with an Introduction by Glenn Sunshine

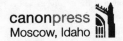
canonpress
Moscow, Idaho

Published by Canon Press
P.O. Box 8729, Moscow, Idaho 83843
800.488.2034 | www.canonpress.com

Stephen Junius Brutus, Vindiciae Contra Tyrannos
This Christian Heritage Series first edition copyright ©2020.
Introduction copyright ©2020 by Dr. Glenn Sunshine.
First published in Latin and French in 1579. Translated into English in 1648.

Cover design by James Engerbretson
Cover illustration by Forrest Dickison
Interior design by Valerie Anne Bost and James Engerbretson
Printed in the United States of America.

Library of Congress Cataloging-in-Publication Data
Languet, Hubert, 1518-1581, author. | Walker, William, active 17th
   century, translator. | Sunshine, Glenn S., 1958- writer of introduction.
   | Languet, Hubert, 1518-1581. Vindiciae contra tyrannos.
Vindiciae contra tyrannos : of the lawful power of the prince over
   the people, and of the people over the prince, being a treatise /
   written by Junius Brutus ; translated by William Walker ; with an
   introduction by Glenn Sunshine.
Vindiciae contra tyrannos. English
First edition. | Moscow, Idaho : Canon Press, 2020. | Series:
   Christian heritage series
LCCN 2020034340 | ISBN 9781952410529 (paperback)
LCSH: Political science--Early works to 1800. | Kings and
   rulers—Duties. | Despotism.
Classification: LCC JC145 .L3513 2020 | DDC 321/.6—dc23
LC record available at https://lccn.loc.gov/2020034340

All rights reserved. No part of this publication may be reproduced, stored in a retrieval system, or transmitted in any form by any means, electronic, mechanical, photocopy, recording, or otherwise, without prior permission of the author, except as provided by USA copyright law.

20 21 22 23 24 25 26 27 28 29   10 9 8 7 6 5 4 3 2

CONTENTS

THE FOURTH QUESTION: *Whether Neighbor Princes May or Are Bound By Law to Aid the Subjects of Other Princes, Persecuted for True Religion, As Oppressed by Manifest Tyranny*

INTRODUCTION

V*indiciae contra tyrannos* ("A Defense of Liberty Against Tyrants," 1579) is a short political treatise written to justify Huguenot resistance against the king of France's attempts to stamp out Protestantism. Despite its brevity, the Vindiciae's sharp defense of the right of subjects to resist unjust or ungodly rulers even to the point of armed rebellion helped shape the political theories of John Locke in England and the American Founding Fathers. Its arguments on the rights and responsibilities of rulers and subjects continue to be relevant today as we consider the limits of the power of the government and the rights of citizens to oppose governmental overreach.

To understand *Vindiciae contra tyrannos*, we need to look at the religious history of France in the sixteenth century. France had been a very Catholic country for centuries, though relations with the papacy were frequently strained. The French king was a quasi-sacred figure, and among other things was obligated in his coronation oaths to fight heresy. That said, Francis I (r.1515-1547) supported church reform as necessary for reforming French society, which allowed various Catholic and Protestant reform programs to arise in competition with

traditional Catholicism. The religious ferment that result-
ed led historian Lucien Fèvre to describe this as a period of
"magnificent religious anarchy."[1]

The Sorbonne—the theological faculty at the University of Paris—
was concerned about this turn of events and did its best to hold heresy
trials, though Francis periodically shut them down due when people
close to the king were accused. That changed, however, in 1534, when
broadsides attacking the Catholic Mass and transubstantiation were
put up in cities across France and even on the king's bedchamber
door in Amboise. The Catholic Church teaches that in the Mass, the
bread and wine used in communion are transubstantiated into the
physical body and blood of Christ. This means that while they retain
their original appearances and properties (e.g., intoxication from the
wine), what you consume is no longer truly bread and wine but Jesus'
body and blood. Protestants viewed this as superstitious nonsense and
derided the Catholic "god of dough" as an idol.

Francis was furious at the posted placards, partly because of the
breach of security at his chateau, but also because transubstantiation
played an unusually important role in France that went well beyond
the theology of the sacrament. In France in this period, the transubstantiated host was a picture of the way power flowed through society,
and thus attacking transubstantiation was tantamount to attacking
royal authority, overturning the social structure, and advocating anarchy.[2] The "placard affair" thus triggered a severe outbreak of persecution that, among other things, drove Calvin out of France and led to
his conversion to Protestantism.

---

1. *A New Kind of History and other essays: Lucien Febvre*, ed. Peter Burke, and trans.
K. Folca (London: Routledge and Kegan Paul, 1973; repr. New York: Harper and
Row, 1973), 85-86.

2. For a complete discussion of this issue, see Christopher Elwood, *The Body
Broken: The Calvinist Doctrine of the Eucharist and the Symbolization of Power in
Sixteenth-Century France* (Oxford University Press, 1999).

The 1540s saw two important developments in French Protestantism. First, Calvin began producing high quality theological writings
in French, the first available in that language. Popular Catholicism
in France had been obsessed with portents of the Antichrist, leaving
people in a state of "prophetic angst." Calvin offered a far more ratio-
nal religious alternative, and so French Protestantism turned increasingly toward Calvin's theology.[3]

Second, Protestantism began to spread through the nobility, including among the Princes of the Blood (i.e., members of the royal
family). This was a dangerous thing: the nobility had military forces
at their disposal that could oppose the king if sufficiently provoked.

Persecution continued under Francis I's son Henry II and under
Henry's sons Francis II and Charles IX, but so did the spread of Protestantism among the nobility. Henry's widow Catherine de Medici was
worried: she wanted stability in France for the sake of her sons, but
the expansion of Protestantism threatened to trigger civil war. To prevent this, her chancellor Michel de l'Hôpital negotiated the Edict of
Saint Germain (1562), which allowed Protestants to worship outside
of towns and the nobles to do so in their town houses. The Catholic
law courts opposed the edict, and when the Duke of Guise, a strongly
Catholic nobleman, encountered a group of Huguenots worshiping according to the terms of the edict in a barn outside of Vassy, he attacked
them, killing about 60 of the 600-700 people present.

When word of the massacre spread, the Protestant nobles mobilized at Orléans and seized other cities in the Loire valley; the royal
army mobilized against them, and this began the first of an inter-
minable series of wars of religion in France. They tended to follow a
pattern: there was a provocation; a war broke out; both sides fought
until a truce was negotiated in which the Protestants were given more
or fewer rights to worship depending on how well they did on the

---

3. See Denis Crouzet, *Les guerriers de Dieu: La violence au temps des troubles des
religion*, vers 1525-vers 1610 (Champ Valon, 1990).

battlefield; and the truce held for a short while until another provocation (often by the Guises) triggered another war.

This was what Catherine de Medici had feared and had tried to avoid. To end the wars, she proposed a dynastic marriage between her daughter Marguerite and Henry Bourbon, the king of Navarre, a Prince of the Blood of France, and the highest born Huguenot leader. The Huguenots agreed, and the Protestants were granted a safe conduct to Paris for the wedding in 1572.

Charles IX was weak-willed like Henry II's other sons. Gaspard de Coligny, the admiral of France and another Huguenot Prince of the Blood, began to have increasing sway over Charles. The Guises were old rivals of Coligny, and they decided to assassinate him during the safe conduct to end his influence at court. The assassination failed; Coligny was severely wounded but survived. The Protestants were understandably furious, and Catherine, Charles IX, and the royal council panicked: they thought that the Protestants in Paris would slaughter the royal family in revenge for the attack on Coligny. The royal council decided to finish off Coligny and to claim that he was conspiring against the king. The rest of the Huguenots were to be reassured that the king held no animosity against them. Henry Guise was sent to dispatch Coligny, but something went wrong: Guise seems to have said that killing Coligny was the king's will, but the town guard interpreted this as a call to kill all the Protestants in the city. The result was the St. Bartholomew's Day Massacres (August 18, 1572).[4] Thousands were killed in Paris, and when news spread, copycat massacres occurred across France. Estimates of the death toll vary from 5,000 to 30,000.

Needless to say, the slaughter triggered another war of religion. It also changed French Protestantism in substantial ways. Many

---

4. Barbara Diefendorf, *Beneath the Cross: Catholics and Huguenots in Sixteenth-Century Paris* (Oxford, 1991) provides a thorough and convincing analysis of the events surrounding the massacres.

Huguenots returned to Catholicism, convinced that the massacres showed that God was not on their side. Of those who remained, the old generation of experienced leaders were now dead, and younger, more hot-headed leaders emerged in the movement. It also meant that the old Huguenot insistence that they were loyal to the king was now unsustainable: it was hard to claim allegiance to a king who was presumed responsible for the slaughter of thousands of your coreligionists during a time of peace.

The result of this was the rise of the so-called Monarchomachs, political theorists who argued for the right to overthrow unjust rulers. Writers such as Theodore Beza, François Hotman, Simon Goulart, Hubert Languet, and Philippe de Mornay addressed the question of when a legitimate king turns into an illegitimate tyrant; to the Huguenots, one obvious answer was when he murdered thousands of his own subjects. The Monarchomachs argued that such as king should be overthrown, some going even so far as to support regicide.

Vindiciae contra Tyrannos was one of the most influential of the Monarchomach treatises. It was written under the pseudonym Stephen Junius Brutus. Scholars differ over its authorship, with Hubert Languet and Philippe de Mornay (or perhaps a collaboration of the two) being the most likely candidates.

The treatise is organized around four questions that get at the heart of the relationship between the king's authority, God's law, and the subjects' responsibilities. Although our circumstances today are very different from those in France 450 years ago, the same kinds of questions are increasingly relevant to an America in which political forces are once again trying to centralize power at the expense of personal liberty and especially religious liberty.

The first question in the *Vindiciae* is whether subjects are obligated to obey princes when they command things contrary to God's law. This is aimed squarely at the emerging theory of the Divine Right of Kings, which argued that it was the subject's duty before God to obey the king even if he ordered things contrary to God's law. If he did, God would judge him, but regardless, it was the subject's duty to obey even such laws. This argument emerged in response to the problem of wars of religion: if God expected people to obey the king in all circumstances, there is no justification for religious war. The author of the *Vindiciae* obviously disagreed, insisting that we must disobey kings who order us to disobey God's law.

The second question is whether subjects are obligated to resist princes when they command things contrary to God's law; the treatise's answer is yes, this was their obligation before God. The third and longest question asks whether and under what circumstances subjects can resist a prince who opposes God's Word. Once again, the answer is yes, but it must be done correctly. This question is the heart of the treatise and includes its most important contributions to political theory. The final question is whether princes must aid subjects of another prince who are persecuted for their faith or are being tyrannically oppressed. The author answers yes to helping those persecuted and gives a qualified yes to aiding subjects of foreign kings.

In these answers, *Vindiciae contra tyrannos* brings together two important threads of Protestant political thought. The first comes from Calvin's political theology. Throughout the middle ages, theologians had argued that kings derived their power from the people, but once the people vested power in the king, it was effectively unalienable: the people did not have a right of rebellion. Calvin took this idea in a different direction. In the book of Exodus, God asked the people of Israel three times if they would accept and live by the terms of the Covenant he was making with them, and three times they said yes before the Covenant went into effect. Calvin saw in this account two critical elements for civil government. First, if God himself required the consent of the people then all government must be based on the consent of the governed. Second, if God set up His government over Israel via a covenant, then all government must consist in a covenant between ruler and ruled.

Following Calvin's thought, *Vindiciae contra tyrannos* argued that legitimate governments are founded on a twofold covenant, first between God on one side and the king and the people on the other in which the king and people agree to obey God, and second between the king and the people in which the people consent to obey the king as long as he rules justly. In this second part of the covenant, the king's coronation oath amounts to a contract with the people. Both parts of the covenant are critical: Should the king disobey God's Word or break his coronation oath, the covenant is broken and the contract between the people and the king becomes null and void just as any other contract would be. In this case, the king may legitimately be resisted without committing sedition.

Although this argument would seem to allow the people the right of revolt, the *Vindiciae* stops short of arguing that. It instead assigns the responsibility to resist the king to the "officers" of the realm, or, to use different terminology, to the lesser or "inferior" magistrates.

This idea is drawn from Luther and is the second major thread of Protestant political thought in the *Vindiciae*. When the Schmalkaldic League was formed by the Lutheran princes in the Holy Roman Empire to defend themselves against Emperor Charles V, they asked Luther for his blessing. He initially refused on the grounds that Romans 13 does not permit them to resist the emperor actively; only passive resistance was legitimate, and even then they must accept the legal consequences of their actions. This was not the answer that the princes expected, and so they sent in the lawyers to talk Luther around. They argued that what Luther said was true in the general case, but that the constitution of the Holy Roman Empire gave the princes the right to oversee the emperor. If he violated his word or did something illegal, the princes were obligated to resist him by the very law of the Empire. After hearing the arguments, Luther wrote the Torgau Memorandum (1530/31) in which he said that if resistance was legal, it was theologically legitimate as well. The common people had no right of rebellion, but lower officers in the civil government—the "inferior" or lesser magistrates—could lead resistance against superior magistrates, even the emperor.

This idea was then generalized to all governments, not just the Holy Roman Empire, and became a core concept in Protestant Resistance Theory, including the *Vindiciae*. Since Huguenot resistance was led by Princes of the Blood, this position made sense: It justified continuing resistance to the monarchy while safeguarding against charges of anarchy.

Implicit in all this is a fundamental idea about government dating back to Augustine of Hippo: because of original sin, no one can be trusted with unlimited power, including kings. All government must therefore be limited, with systems of checks and balances to prevent anyone from overstepping his legitimate powers.[5] Protestant Resistance Theory in effect argued that the right of resistance by the lesser magistrate was a necessary part of the system of checks and balances required by good government.

Although the *Vindiciae* expressly advocated for resistance to tyranny led by the lesser magistrate, the logic of its position supported the idea that the people themselves had a right to oppose unjust rulers based on each person's covenantal relationship with God.[6] As a result, the Vindiciae was translated into English in 1648 during the English Civil War and became an important influence on English political thought. The Puritans then brought that thinking to the New World, where it became deeply embedded in New England's political philosophy. Remarkably, John Adams' *Defence* [sic] *of the Constitution of the*

---

5. We often think that the concept of checks and balances originated with the U.S. Constitution, but they were in place in all medieval governments due to the influence of Augustine's *The City of God*.

6. George Buchanan's *De Jure Regni apud Scotos* (1579) was the first Protestant treatise to argue that the people themselves have the right of resistance and thus that they could revolt against the government even without the support of the lesser magistrate.

United States of America listed the *Vindiciae* as one of the key works produced in England(!) that dealt with problems of tyranny and limited government. This was a mark of its influence not only on English political thought, but Adams' as well.[7]

Discussions of the American Founders often ignore the profound influence of Calvinist political theories on the Revolution. Covenantal theories of government, the definition of tyranny as the violation of the social contract, and above all the right of resistance to tyranny—all ideas found in the *Vindiciae*—were the foundation of political life in New England, the cradle of the Revolution. Most discussion of the Founders' ideas has instead focused on the more abstract natural rights theory found in Thomas Jefferson and the Declaration of Independence, yet even this was shaped by the *Vindiciae* as mediated by Locke. If we are to understand the political theory that motivated the American Founders, we thus need to study not just Locke's *Second Treatise on Civil Government* but works like *Vindiciae contra tyrannos* as representative of Protestant Resistance Theory and the Calvinist political tradition.

Most importantly, given the times in which we live, the *Vindiciae* provides us with a valuable perspective on the power of the state and the rights of citizens. Since it was written in very different historical circumstances from our own, it is not subject to the blinders and preconceptions of our own age and so can help us see past them. Even though we might not agree with all of the *Vindiciae*'s conclusions, we can still benefit from its clarity of thought and its challenge to live faithfully without compromise as we face the challenges of our own era.

GLENN SUNSHINE

---

7. Stanley Bamberg, "A Footnote to the Political Theory of John Adams *Vindiciae contra tyrannos*," 1996. https://www.libertypost.org/cgi-bin/readart. cgi?ArtNum=27906

DEDICATION AND EPISTLE

The Emperors Theodosias and Valentinian to Volusianus, great provost of the empire.

It is a thing well becoming the majesty of an Emperor to acknowledge himself bound to obey the laws. Our authority depending on the authority of the laws, and in very deed to submit the principality to law, is a greater thing than to bear rule. We therefore make it known unto all men, by the declaration of this our edict, that we do not allow ourselves, or repute it lawful, to do anything contrary to this.

Justin in the Second Book, speaks thus of Lycurgus, Lawgiver to the Lacedemonians: he gave laws to the Spartans which had not any; and was as much renowned for his diligent observing of them himself, as for his discreet inventing of them. For he made no laws for others, to the obedience whereof he did not first submit himself: fashioning the people to obey willingly, and the prince to govern uprightly.

THE FIRST QUESTION

Whether subjects are bound and ought to obey princes, if they command
that which is against the law of God.

This question happily may seem at the first view to be altogether superfluous and unprofitable, for that it seems to make a doubt of an axiom always held infallible amongst Christians, confirmed by many testimonies in Holy Scripture, divers examples of the histories of all ages, and by the death of all the holy martyrs. For it may be well demanded wherefore Christians have endured so many afflictions, but that they were always persuaded that God must be obeyed simply and absolutely, and kings with this exception, that they command not that which is repugnant to the law of God. In another way, wherefore, should the apostles have answered that God must rather be obeyed than men, and also seeing that the only will of God is always just and that of men may be, and is, oftentimes unjust, who can doubt but that we must always obey God's commandments without any exception, and men's ever with limitation?

But forsomuch as there are many princes in these days, calling themselves Christians, which arrogantly assume an unlimited power, over which God himself hath no command, and that they have no want of flatterers which adore them as gods upon earth, many others also, which for fear or by constraint either seem or else do believe that princes ought to be obeyed in all things and by all men. And withal, seeing the unhappiness of these times is such, that there is nothing so firm, certain, or pure which is not shaken, disgraced, or polluted, I fear me that whosoever shall nearly and thoroughly consider these things will confess this question to be not only most profitable, but also, the times considered, most necessary. For my own part, when I consider the cause of the many calamities wherewith Christendom hath been afflicted for these late years, I cannot but remember that of the prophet Hosea, "the princes of Judah were like them that remove the bounds: wherefore I will pour out myself like water. Ephraim is oppressed and broken in judgment, because he willingly walked after the commandments" (5:10-11). Here you see the sin of the princes and people dispersed in these two words. The princes exceed their bounds, not contenting themselves with that authority which the almighty and all good God hath given them, but seek to usurp that sovereignty which He hath reserved to himself over all men, being not content to command the bodies and goods of their subjects at their pleasure, but assume license to themselves to enforce the consciences, which appertains chiefly to Jesus Christ. Holding the earth not great enough for their ambition, they will climb and conquer heaven itself. The people on the other side walk after the commandment when they yield to the desire of princes, who command them that which is against the law of God, and as it were to burn incense and adore these earthly gods, and instead of resisting them, if they have means and occasion, suffer them to usurp the place of God, making no conscience to give that to Caesar which belongs properly and only to God.

Now is there any man that sees not this: if a man disobey a prince commanding that which is wicked and unlawful, he shall presently be esteemed a rebel, a traitor, and guilty of high treason. Our Savior Christ, the apostles, and all the Christians of the primitive church were charged with these calumnies. If any, after the example of Ezra and Nehemiah, dispose himself to the building of the temple of the Lord, it will be said he aspires to the crown, hatches innovations, and seeks the ruin of the state. Then you shall presently see a million of these minions and flatterers of princes tickling their ears with an opinion: that if they once suffer this temple to be re-builded, they may bid their kingdom farewell and never look to raise impost or taxes on these men.

But what a madness is this! There are no estates which ought to be esteemed firm and stable but those in whom the temple of God is built, and which are indeed the temple itself, and these we may truly call kings, which reign with God, seeing that it is by him only that kings reign. On the contrary, what beastly foolishness it is to think that the state and kingdom cannot subsist if God Almighty be not excluded and his temple demolished. From hence proceeds so many tyrannous enterprises, unhappy and tragic death of kings, and ruins of people. If these sycophants knew what difference there is between God and Caesar, between the King of kings and a simple king, between the lord and the vassal, and what tributes this lord requires of his subjects and what authority he gives to kings over those his subjects, certainly so many princes would not strive to trouble the kingdom of God and we should not see some of them precipitated from their thrones by the just instigation of the Almighty, revenging Himself of them in the midst of their greatest strength, and the people should not be sacked and pillaged and trodden down.

It then belongs to princes to know how far they may extend their authority, and to subjects in what they may obey them, lest the one encroaching on that jurisdiction which no way belongs to them, and the others obeying him which commands further than he ought, they be both chastised when they shall give an account thereof before another judge. Now the end and scope of the question propounded, whereof the Holy Scripture shall principally give the resolution, is that which follows. The question is if subjects be bound to obey kings

in case they command that which is against the law of God, that is
to say, to which of the two (God or king) must we rather obey, when
the question shall be resolved concerning the king, to whom is attributed absolute power, that concerning other magistrates shall be
also determined.

First, the Holy Scripture does teach that God reigns by his own
proper authority and kings by derivation, God from Himself, kings
from God, that God hath a jurisdiction proper, kings are His dele-
gates. It follows then that the jurisdiction of God hath no limits, that
of kings bounded; that the power of God is infinite, that of kings
confined; that the kingdom of God extends itself to all places, that
of kings is restrained within the confines of certain countries. In
like manner God hath created of nothing both heaven and earth;
wherefore by good right He is lord and true proprietor, both of the
one and the other. All the inhabitants of the earth hold of Him that
which they have, and are but His tenants and farmers; all the princes
and governors of the world are His stipendiaries and vassals and are
bound to take and acknowledge their investitures from Him. Briefly,
God alone is the owner and lord, and all men of what degree or quality soever they be, are His servants, farmers, officers and vassals, and
owe account and acknowledgment to Him, according to that which
He hath committed to their dispensation; the higher their place is the
greater their account must be, and according to the ranks whereunto
God hath raised them must they make their reckoning before His divine majesty, which the Holy Scriptures teaches in infinite places, and
all the faithful, yea, and the wisest among the heathen have ever acknowledged. The earth is the Lord's, and the fullness thereof (so saith
king David, Ps. 24:1). And to the end that men should not sacrifice
to their own industry, the earth yields no increase without the dew
of heaven. Wherefore God commanded that His people should offer
unto Him the first of their fruits, and the heathens themselves hath
consecrated the same unto their gods, to the end that God might

be acknowledged lord, and they His grangers and vine dressers; the heaven is the throne of the Lord, and the earth His footstool.

And, therefore, seeing all the kings of the world are under his feet, it is no marvel if God be called the King of kings and Lord of lords; all kings be termed His ministers established to judge rightly and govern justly the world in the quality of lieutenants. "By me," so says the divine wisdom, "kings reign, and the princes judge the earth" (Prov. 8:15). If they do it not He looses the bonds of kings and girds their loins with a girdle (Job 12:18), as if He should say it is in my power to establish kings in their thrones, or to thrust them out, and from that occasion the throne of kings is called the throne of God. "Blessed be the Lord thy God," says the Queen of Sheba to King Solomon, "which delighted in you to set you on his throne to be king for the Lord thy God, to do judgment and justice" (1 Kings 10:9). In like manner we read in another place that Solomon sat on the throne of the Lord, or on the throne of the Lord's kingdom.

By the same reason the people are always called the Lord's people, and the Lord's inheritance, and the king's governor of this inheritance, and conductor or leader of his people of God, which is the title given to David, to Solomon, to Hezekiah and to other good princes; when also the covenant is passed between God and the king, it is upon condition that the people be, and remain always, the people of God, to show that God will not in any case despoil himself of his property and possession, when he gives to kings the government of the people, but establish them to take charge of, and well use them, no more nor less than he which makes choice of a shepherd to look to his flocks, remains, notwithstanding himself, still master and owner of them.

This was always known to those good kings, David, Solomon, Jehoshaphat, and others who acknowledged God to be the lord of their kingdoms and nations, and yet lost no privilege that justly belongs to real power; yea, they reigned much more happily in that they employed themselves cheerfully in the service of God and in obedience to his commandments. Nebuchadnezzar, although he was a heathen and a mighty emperor, did yet at the end acknowledge this, for though Daniel called him the king of kings, to whom the King of Heaven had granted power and royal majesty above all others, yet on the contrary, said he, "Thy God, O Daniel, is truly the God of Gods, and Lord of lords," giving kingdoms to whom He pleases (Dan. 2:47), yea, to the most wretched of the world. For which cause Xenophon said at the coronation of Cyrus, "Let us sacrifice to God." And profane writers in many places do magnify God the most mighty and sovereign king. At this day at the inaugurating of kings and Christian princes, they are called the servants of God, destined to govern His people. Seeing then that kings are only the lieutenants of God, established in the Throne of God by the Lord God himself, and the people are the people of God, and that the honor which is done to these lieutenants proceeds from the reverence which is born to those that sent them to this service, it follows of necessity that kings must be obeyed for God's cause, and not against God, and then, when they serve and obey God, and not otherwise.

It may be that the flatterers of the court will reply that God has resigned His power unto kings, reserving heaven for himself, and allowing the earth to them to reign and govern there according to their own fancies; briefly that the great ones of the world hold a divided empire with God himself. Behold a discourse proper enough for that impudent villain Cleon the sycophant of Alexander, or for the poet Martial, which was not ashamed to call the edicts of Domitian the ordinances of the Lord God. This discourse, I say, is worthy of that execrable Domitian who (as Suetonius recites) would be called god and lord. But altogether unworthy of the ears of a Christian prince and of the mouth of good subjects that sentence of God Almighty must always remain irrevocably true: "I will not give My glory to any other," (42:8) that is, no man shall have such absolute authority, but I will always remain sovereign.

God does not at any time divest Himself of His power; He holds a scepter in one hand to repress and quell the audacious boldness of those princes who mutiny against Him, and in the other a balance to control those who administer not justice with equity as they ought; than these there cannot be expressed more certain marks of sovereign command. And if the emperor, in creating a king, reserves always to himself the imperial sovereignty, or a king, as he of France, in granting the government or possession of a province to a stranger, or if it be to his brother or son, reserves always to himself appeals and the knowledge of such things as are the marks of royalty and sovereignty, the which also are always understood of themselves to be excepted, although they were altogether omitted in the grant of investiture and fealty promised; with much more reason should God have sovereign power and command over all kings being His servants and officers, seeing we read in so many places of Scripture that He will call them to an account and punish them if they do not faithfully discharge their duties. Then therefore all kings are the vassals of the King of kings, invested into their office by the sword, which is the cognizance of their royal authority, to the end that with the sword they maintain the law of God, defend the good, and punish the evil. Even as we commonly see that he who is a sovereign lord puts his vassals into possession of their fee by girding them with a sword, delivering them a buckler and a standard, with condition that they shall fight for them with those arms if occasion shall serve.

Now if we consider what is the duty of vassals, we shall find that what may be said of them, agrees properly to kings. The vassal receives his fee of his lord with right of justice, and charge to serve him in his wars. The king is established by the Lord God, the King of kings, to the end he should administer justice to his people and defend them against all their enemies. The vassal receives laws and conditions from his sovereign. God commands the king to observe His laws and to have them always before his eyes, promising that he and his successors shall possess long the kingdom if they be obedient, and on the contrary that their reign shall be of small continuance if they prove rebellious to their sovereign king. The vassal obliges himself by oath unto his lord, and swears that he will be faithful and obedient. In like manner the king promises solemnly to command, according to the express law of God. Briefly, the vassal loses his fee if he commit a felony, and by law forfeits all his privileges. In the like case the king loses his right, and many times his realm also, if he despise God, if he complot with His enemies, and if he commit felony against that royal majesty. This will appear more clearly by the consideration of the covenant which is contracted between God and the king, for God does that honor to His servants to call them His confederates. Now we read of two sorts of covenants at the inaugurating of kings, the first between God, the king, and the people, that the people might be the people of God; the second, between the king and the people, that the people shall obey faithfully, and the king command justly. We will treat hereafter of the second, and now speak of the first.

When King Joash was crowned, we read that a covenant was contracted between God, the king, and the people, or, as it is said in another place, between Jehoiada the high priest, all the people, and the king, that God should be their lord (2 Kings 11:17.) In like manner we read that Josiah and all the people entered into covenants with the Lord: we may gather from these testimonies that in passing these covenants the high priest did covenant in the name of God in express terms, that the king and the people should take order that God might be served purely and according to His will throughout the whole kingdom of Judah, that the king should so reign that the people were suffered to serve God and held in obedience to his law. Thus the people should so obey the king, as their obedience should have principal relation to God. It appears by this that the king and the people are jointly bound by promise and did oblige themselves by solemn oath to serve God before all things. And indeed presently after they had sworn the covenant, Josiah and Joash did ruin the idolatry of Baal and re-established the pure service of God. The principal points of the covenants were chiefly these: that the king himself, and all the people should be careful to honor and serve God according to His will revealed in His word, which, if they performed, God would assist and preserve their estates, as in doing the contrary He would abandon and exterminate them, which does plainly appear by the conferring of divers passages of holy writ.

Moses, somewhat before his death, propounds these conditions of covenant to all the people, and at the same time commands that the law, which are those precepts given by the Lord, should be in deposit kept in the ark of the covenant. After the decease of Moses, Joshua was established captain and conductor of the people of God, and according as the Lord Himself admonished, if he would have happy success in his affairs, he should not in any sort estrange himself from the law. Joshua also, for his part, desiring to make the Israelites understand upon what condition God had given them the country of Canaan, as soon as they were entered into it, after due sacrifices performed, he read the law in the presence of all the people, promising unto them in the Lord's name all good things if they persisted in obedience, and threatening of all evil if they willfully connived in disobedience. Summarily, he assures them all prosperity if they observed the law, as otherwise he expressly declared that in doing the contrary they should be utterly ruined. Also at all such times as they left the service of God, they were delivered into the hands of the Canaanites and reduced into slavery under their tyranny.

Now this covenant between God and the people in the times of the judges had vigor also in the times of the kings, and was treated with them. After that Saul had been anointed, chosen, and wholly established king, Samuel speaks unto the people in these terms: "Behold the king whom you have demanded and chosen; God hath established him king over you; obey you therefore and serve the Lord,

as well as your king which is established over you, otherwise you and
your king shall perish" (1 Sam. 12), as if he should say, you would
have a king, and God has given you this here; notwithstanding think
not that God will suffer any encroachment upon His right, but know
that the king is as well bound to observe the law as you, and if he fail
therein, his delinquency shall be punished as severely as yours. Briefly,
according to your desires Saul is given you for your king, to lead you
in the wars, but with this condition annexed: that he himself follow
the law of God. After that Saul was rejected because he kept not his
promise; David was established king on the same condition; so also
was his son Solomon, for the Lord said, "If you keep my law, I will
confirm with you the covenant which I contracted with David" (2
Chron. 7:18). Now concerning this covenant, it is inserted into the
second book of the Chronicles, as follows. "There shall not fail you
a man in my sight to sit upon the throne of Israel: yet so that thy
children take heed to their way to walk in my law, as you hast walked
before me. But if they serve idols, I will drive them from the land
whereof I have given them possession" (2 Chron. 7). And therefore it
was that the book of the law was called the book of the covenant of
the Lord (who commanded the priests to give it the king), according
to which Samuel put it into the hands of Saul, and according to the
tenure thereof Josiah yields himself feudatory and vassal of the Lord.
Also the law which is kept in the ark is called the covenant of the
Lord with the children of Israel. Finally, the people delivered from
the captivity of Babylon do renew the covenant with God, and do
acknowledge throughout the chapter that they worthily deserved all
those punishments for their falsifying their promise to God (Ezra
10). It appears, then, that the kings swear as vassals to observe the law
of God, whom they confess to be sovereign lord over all.

Now, according to that which we have already touched, if they violate their oath and transgress the law, we say that they have lost their
kingdom as vassals lose their fee by committing felony. We have said

that there was the same covenant between God and the kings of Judah, as before, between God and the people in the times of Joshua and the judges. But we see in many places that when the people has despised the law or made covenants with Baal, God has delivered them into the hands of Eglon, Jabin, and other kings of the Canaanites. And as it is one and the same covenant, so those who do break it receive like punishment. Saul is so audacious to sacrifice, infringing thereby the law of God, and presently after saves the life of Agag, king of the Amalekites, against the express commandment of God. For this occasion he is called rebel by Samuel, and finally is chastised for his rebellion. "You have sacrificed," saith he, "but you hadst done better to obey God, for obedience is more worthy than sacrifice. you hast neglected the Lord thy God, He also has rejected you, that you reign no more over Israel" (1 Sam. 15:22-23). This has been so certainly observed by the Lord that the very children of Saul were deprived of their paternal inheritance, for that he, having committed high treason, did thereby incur the punishment of tyrants which affect a kingdom that no way appertains unto them. And not only the kings, but also their children and successors have been deprived of the kingdom by reason of such felony. Solomon revolted from God to worship idols. Incontinently the prophet Ahijah foretells that the kingdom shall be divided under his son Rehoboam. Finally, the word of the Lord is accomplished, and ten tribes, who made the greatest portion of the kingdom, do quit Rehoboam, and adhere to Jeroboam his servant.

Wherefore is this? "Forsomuch," says the Lord, "that they have left me to go after Ashtaroth, the god of the Sidonians and Chemosh, the god of the Moabites, etc. I will also break in pieces their kingdom," as if He should say, 'they have violated the covenant, and have not kept promise; I am no more then tied unto them. They will lessen my majesty, and I will lessen their kingdom. Although they be my servants, yet notwithstanding they will expel me my kingdom. But I will drive them out themselves by Jeroboam, who is their servant.' Furthermore, forsomuch as this servant, fearing that the ten tribes, for the cause of religion should return to Jerusalem, set up calves in Bethel, and made Israel to sin, withdrawing by this means the people far from God, what was the punishment of so ungrateful a vassal and wicked traitor towards his Lord? First, his son died and in the end all his race, even unto the last of the males, was taken from the face of the earth by the sword of Baasha, according to the judgment which was pronounced against him by the prophet, because he revolted from the obedience of the Lord God; this, then, is cause sufficient and oftentimes also propounded, for the which God does take from the king his fee, when he opposes the law of God and withdraws himself from Him to follow His enemies, to wit, idols and as like crimes deserve like punishments, we read in the holy histories that kings of Israel and of Judah who have so far forgotten themselves have in the end miserably perished.

Now, although the form, both of the church and the Jewish kingdom be changed, for that which was before enclosed within the narrow bounds of Judea is now dilated throughout the whole world, notwithstanding the same things may be said of Christian kings, the gospel having succeeded the law, and Christian princes being in the place of those of Jewry. There is the same covenant, the same conditions, the same punishments, and if they fail in the accomplishing, the same God Almighty, revenger of all perfidious disloyalty, and as the former were bound to keep the law, so the other are obliged to adhere to the doctrine of the Gospel, for the advancement whereof these kings at their anointing and receiving do promise to employ the utmost of their means.

Herod, fearing Christ, whose reign he should rather have desired, sought to put Him to death, as if He had affected a kingdom in this world, did himself miserably perish and lost his kingdom. Julian the apostate did cast off Christ Jesus to cleave unto the impiety and idolatry of the pagans, but within a small time after he fell to his confusion through the force of the arm of Christ, whom in mockery he called the Galilean. Ancient histories are replete with such examples; neither is there any want in those of these times. Of late years divers kings, drunk with the liquor which the whore of Babylon has presented unto them, have taken arms and for the love of the wolf and of Antichrist have made war against the Lamb of God, who is Christ Jesus, and yet at this day some amongst them do continue in the same course. We have seen some of them ruined in the deed and in the midst of their wickedness; others also carried from their triumphs to their graves. Those who survive and follow them in their courses have little reason to expect a better issue of their wicked practices: this sentence remains always most certain: that "though all the kings of the earth do conjure and conspire against Christ and endeavor to cut in pieces our Lamb, yet in the end they shall yield the place, and maugre their hearts, confess that this Lamb is the King of kings, and Lord of lords."

But what shall we say of the heathen kings? Certainly although they be not anointed and sacred of God, yet be they His vassals and have received their power from Him, whether they be chosen by lot or any other means whatsoever. If they have been chosen by the voices of an assembly, we say that God governs the heart of man and addresses the minds and intentions of all persons whither He pleases. If it be by lot, the lot is cast in the lap, saith the wise man, "but the whole disposing thereof is of the Lord" (Prov. 16:33). It is God only that in all ages establishes and takes away, confirms and overthrows kings according to His good pleasure. In which regard Isaiah calls Cyrus the anointed of the Lord (Is. 45:1), and Daniel says that Nebuchadnezzar and others have had their kingdoms committed unto them by God (Dan. 4:17), as also Saint Paul maintains that all magistrates have received their authority from Him (Rom. 13:1). For, although that God has not commanded pagans in express terms to obey Him as He has done those who have knowledge of Him, yet notwithstanding the pagans must needs confess that it is by the sovereign God that they reign;

wherefore if they will not yield the tribute that they owe to God in regard of themselves, at the least let them not attempt nor hinder the sovereign to gather that which is due from those people who are in subjection to them; nor that they do not anticipate nor appropriate to themselves divine jurisdiction over them, which is the crime of high treason and true tyranny, for which occasion the Lord has grievously punished even the pagan kings themselves. It then becomes those princes who will free themselves from so enormous a mischief carefully to distinguish their jurisdiction from that of God's, yea, so much the more circumspectly for that God and the prince have their right of authority over one and the same land, over one and the same man, over one and the same thing. Man is composed of body and soul; God has formed the body and infused the soul into him; to Him only then may be attributed and appropriated the commands both over the body and soul of man.

If out of His mere grace and favor He has permitted kings to employ both the bodies and goods of their subjects, yet still with this proviso and charge: that they preserve and defend their subjects. Certainly kings ought to think that the use of this authority is in such manner permitted, notwithstanding that the abuse of it is absolutely forbidden. First, those who confess that they hold their souls and lives of God, as they ought to acknowledge, they have then no right to impose any tribute upon souls. The king takes tribute and custom of the body and of such things as are acquired or gained by the industry and travail of the body. God does principally exact His right from the soul, which also in part executes her functions by the body. In the tribute of the king are comprehended the fruits of the earth, the contributions of money and other charges, both real and personal; the tribute of God is in prayers, sacraments, predications of the pure Word of God; briefly, all that which is called divine service, as well private as public. These two tributes are in such manner divers and distinguished that the one hurts not the other. The exchequer of God takes nothing from that of Caesar, but each of them have their right manifestly apart. But to speak in a word, whosoever confounds these things, confounds heaven and earth together and endeavors to reduce them into their first chaos, or latter confusion. David hath excellently well distinguished these affairs, ordaining officers to look to the right of God, and others for that of the king. Jehoshaphat has followed the same course, establishing certain persons to judge the causes that belonged to the Almighty, and others to look to the justice of the king; the one to maintain the pure service of God, the other to preserve the rights of the king. But if a prince usurp the right of God and put himself forward after the manner of the giants to scale the heavens, he is no less guilty of high treason to his sovereign and commits felony in the same manner, as if one of his vassals should seize on the rights of his crown and put himself into evident danger to be despoiled of his estates, and that so much the more justly, there being no proportion between God and an earthly king, between the Almighty and a mortal man, whereas yet between the lord and the vassal there is some relation of proportion.

So often, therefore, as any prince shall so much forget himself as insolently to say in his heart, 'I will ascend into heaven, I will exalt my throne above the stars of God; I will sit also upon the mount of the congregation in the sides of the north; I will ascend above the heights of the clouds, I will be like the Most High,' then on the contrary will the Almighty say, 'I will rise up more high, I will set myself against you; I will erase out thy name and all thy posterity, thy counsels shall vanish into smoke, but that which I have once determined shall remain firm, and never be annihilated.' The Lord said unto Pharaoh, "Let My people go, that they may serve Me, and offer sacrifice unto Me," and for that this proud man answered that he knew not the God of the Hebrews, presently after he was miserably destroyed. Nebuchadnezzar commanded that his statue should be adored and would be honored as God, but within a short time the true God did

deservedly chastise his unruly boldness, and desiring to be accounted
God, he became a brute beast, wandering through desert places like
a wild ass, until, says the prophet, he acknowledged the God of Israel
to be the sovereign Lord over all; his son Belshazzar abused the holy
vessels of the temple in Jerusalem, and put them to serve his excess
and drunkenness, for he gave not glory to Him that held in His hands
both his soul and his counsels; he lost his kingdom and was slain in
that very night of feasting.

Alexander the Great took pleasure in the lies of his flatterers, who
termed him the son of Jupiter, and not only approved but procured
his adoration, but a sudden death gave a sad period to those triumphs,
being blinded through his excess of conquests he began with too
much affection to delight in. Antiochus, under color of pacifying and
uniting his subjects, commanded all men to forsake the laws of God
and to apply themselves in obedience to his; he profaned the temple
of the Jews and polluted their altars, but after divers ruins, defeats,
and loss of battles, despoiled and disgraced, he dies with grief, confessing that he deservedly suffered those miseries, because he would
have constrained the Jews to leave their religion. If we take into our
consideration the death of Nero, that inhuman butcherer of Christians, whom he unjustly slandered with the firing of Rome, being the
abhorred act of his detested self; the end of Caligula, which made
himself to be adored; of Domitian who would be called lord and god;
of Commodus, and divers others who would appropriate to themselves the honors due to God alone, we shall find that they have all
and always according to their deceits miserably perished; when, on
the contrary, Trajan, Adrian, Antonius the courteous, and others have
finished their days in peace, for although they knew not the true God,
yet have they permitted the Christians the exercise of their religion.

Briefly, even as those rebellious vassals who endeavor to possess
themselves of the kingdom do commit felony by the testimony of all
laws and deserve to be extirpated, in like manner those are as really

guilty which will not observe the divine law, whereunto all men without exception owe their obedience, or who persecute those who desire to conform themselves thereunto without hearing them in their just defenses. Now since we see that God invests kings into their kingdoms, almost in the same manner that vassals are invested into their fees by their sovereign, we must needs conclude that kings are the vassals of God and deserve to be deprived of the benefit they receive from their lord if they commit felony, in the same fashion as rebellious vassals are of their estates. These premises being allowed, this question may be easily resolved; for if God hold the place of sovereign lord, and the king as vassal, who dare deny but that we must rather obey the sovereign than the vassal? If God commands one thing and the king commands the contrary, what is that proud man that would term him a rebel who refuses to obey the king, when else he must disobey God? But, on the contrary, he should rather be condemned and held for truly rebellious who omits to obey God, or who will obey the king, when he forbids him to yield obedience to God.

Briefly, if God calls us on the one side to enroll us in His service, and the king on the other, is any man so void of reason that he will not say we must leave the king and apply ourselves to God's service? So far be it from us to believe that we are bound to obey a king commanding anything contrary to the law of God that, contrarily, in obeying him we become rebels to God, no more nor less than we would esteem a countryman a rebel who, for the love he bears to some rich and ancient inferior lord, would bear arms against the sovereign prince, or who had rather obey the writs of an inferior judge than of a superior, the commandments of a lieutenant of a province than of a prince; to be brief, the directions of an officer rather than the express ordinances of the king himself. In doing this we justly incur the malediction of the prophet Micah, who does detest and curse in the name of God all those who obey the wicked and perverse ordinances of kings. By the law of God we understand the two tables given to

Moses, in the which, as in unremovable bounds, the authority of all princes ought to be fixed. The first comprehends that which we owe to God, the second that which we must do to our neighbors; briefly, they contain piety and justice conjoined with charity, from which the preaching of the gospel does not derogate, but rather authorize and confirm. The first table is esteemed the principal, as well in order as in dignity. If the prince commands to cut the throat of an innocent, to pillage and commit extortion, there is no man (provided he has some feeling of conscience) who would execute such a commandment. If the prince has committed some crime, such as adultery, parricide, or some other wickedness, behold amongst the heathen, the learned lawyer Papinian who will reprove Caracalla to his face and had rather die than obey when his cruel prince commands him to lie and palliate his offence; nay, although he threaten him with a terrible death, yet would he not bear false witness. What shall we do then, if the prince command us to be idolaters, if he would have us again crucify Christ Jesus, if he enjoins us to blaspheme and despise God, and to drive Him (if it were possible) out of heaven, is there not yet more reason to disobey him, than to yield obedience to such extravagant commands? Yet a little farther, seeing it is not sufficient to abstain from evil, but that we must do good, instead of worshiping of idols, we must adore and serve the true God, according as He has commanded us, and instead of bending our knees before Baal, we must render to the Lord the honor and service which He requires of us. For we are bound to serve God for His own sake only, but we honor our prince and love our neighbor, because and for the love of God.

Now if it be ill done to offend our neighbor, and if it be a capital crime to rise against our prince, how shall we entitle those who rise in rebellion against the majesty of the sovereign Lord of all mankind. Briefly, as it is a thing much more grievous to offend the creator, than the creature; man than the image he represents; and as in the terms of law, he that has wounded the proper person of a king is much more culpable than another who has only broken the statue erected in his memory, so there is no question but a much more terrible punishment is prepared for them who infringe the first table of the law than for those who only sin against the second, although the one depend on the other; whereupon it follows (to speak by comparison) that we must take more careful regard of the observation of the first than of the second.

Furthermore, our progenitors' examples may teach us the rule we must follow in this case. King Ahab, at the instigation of his wife Jezebel, killed all the prophets and servants of God that could be taken, notwithstanding, Obadiah, steward of Ahab's house, did both hide and feed in a cave a hundred prophets; the excuse for this is soon ready: in obligations, oblige they never so nearly, the Divine Majesty must always be excepted. The same Ahab enjoined all men to sacrifice to Baal. Elijah, instead of cooling or relenting, did reprove more freely the king and all the people, convinced the priests of Baal of their impiety, and caused them to be executed. Then, in despite of that wicked and furious Jezebel, and maugre that uxorious king, he does redress and reform with a divine and powerful endeavor the service of the true God. When Ahab reproached him (as the princes of our times do) that he troubled Israel, that he was rebellious, seditious, titles wherewith they are ordinarily charged, who are no way culpable thereof, nay, but it is you thyself, answered Elijah, who by thy apostasy has troubled Israel, who has left the Lord, the true God, to acquaint thyself with strange gods His enemies (1 Kings 18:18). In the same manner and by the leading and direction of the same spirit did Shadrach, Meshach, and Abednego refuse to obey Nebuchadnezzar, Daniel, Darius, Eleazar, Antiochus, and infinite others. After the coming of Jesus Christ, it being forbidden the apostles to preach the gospel, "Judge ye," said they, "whether it be reasonable as in the sight of God to obey men, rather than God" (Acts 4:19); according to this, the apostles, not regarding either the intendments or designs of the greatness of the world, addressed themselves readily to do that which their master, Jesus Christ, had commanded them.

The Jews themselves would not permit that there should be set up in the temple at Jerusalem the eagle of silver, nor the statue of Caligula; what did Ambrose when the Emperor Valentinian commanded him to give the temple at Milan to the Arians? "Thy counselors and captains are come unto me," said he, "to make me speedily deliver the temple, saying it was done by the authority and command of the emperor, and that all things are in his power. I answered to it that if he demanded that which is mine, to wit, mine inheritance, my money, I would not in any sort refuse it him, although all my goods belong properly to the poor, but the things divine are not in subjection to the power of the emperor." What do we think that this holy man would have answered if he had been demanded whether the living temple of the Lord should be enthralled to the slavery of idols? These examples and the constancy of a million martyrs who were glorious in their deaths for not yielding obedience in this kind, according as the Ecclesiastical Histories, which are full of them, do demonstrate, may sufficiently serve for an express law in this case.

But for all this we have no want of a law formerly written. For as often and ever as the apostles admonish Christians to obey kings and magistrates, they do first exhort, and as it were by way of advice, admonish everyone to subject himself in like manner to God, and to obey Him before and against any whatsoever, and there is nowhere to be found in any of their writings the least passage for this unlimited obedience which the flatterers of princes do exact from men of small understandings. "Let every soul," saith Saint Paul, "be subject to the higher powers, for there is no power but of God" (Rom. 13:1). He makes mention of every soul to the end it may not be thought that he would exempt any from this subjection; we may easily gather by divers such speeches that we must obey God rather than the king. For if we obey the king, because and for the love of God, certainly this obedience may not be a conspiracy against God. But the apostle will stop the gap to all ambiguity in adding that the prince is the servant of God for our good, to wit, to do justice; from this necessarily follows that which we come from touching, that we must rather obey God than him who is His servant. This does not yet content Saint Paul, for he adds in the end, "Give tribute, honor, and fear to whom they appertain," (Rom. 13:7) as if he should say, that which was alleged by Christ, " Give to Caesar that which is Caesar's, and to God that which is God's" (Matt. 22:21): to Caesar tribute, and honor; to God, fear. Saint Peter says the same, "Fear God, honor the king; servants, obey your masters, not only the good and kind, but also the rigorous" (1 Pet. 2:17). We must practice these precepts according to the order they are set down in: to wit, that as servants are not bound to obey their masters if they command anything which is against the laws and ordinances of kings, subjects in like manner owe no obedience to kings which will make them to violate the law of God.

Certain lewd companions object that even in the things themselves that concern the conscience we must obey kings and are so shameless as to produce for witness of so wicked an opinion the apostles Saint Peter and Saint Paul, concluding from hence that we must yield obedience to all that the king shall ordain, though it be to embrace, without reply, any superstition he shall please to establish. But there is no man so grossly void of sense that sees not the impiety of these men. We reply that Saint Paul says in express terms we must be subject to princes, not only for wrath, but also for conscience sake. In opposing conscience to wrath, it is as much as if the apostle had said that the obedience of which he speaks ought not to proceed for fear of punishment, but from the love of God, and from the reverence which we are bound to bear unto the Word. In the same sense Saint Paul enjoins servants in such manner to obey their masters that it be not with eye service for fear of stripes, but in singleness of heart, fearing God, not simply to acquire the favor of men, whom they may delude, but to bear the burden laid on their shoulders by Him whom no man can deceive.

In brief there is manifest difference between these two manners of speech: to obey, for conscience sake, and to obey in those things which concern the conscience; otherwise those who had much rather lose their lives with infinite torments than obey princes who command them things contrary to the will of God would have taught us that which these seek to persuade us to. Neither do they express themselves less impudent in that which they are accustomed to object to those who are not so well able to answer them. That obedience is better than sacrifice, for there is no text in Holy Writ that does more evidently confound them than this which is contained in Samuel's reprehension of King Saul for his disobedience to the commandment of God in sacrificing unfittingly. If then Saul, although he were a king, ought to obey God, it follows in all good consequence that subjects are not bound to obey their king by offending of God. Briefly those who (after the barbarous manner of the men of Calcutta) seek to enthrall the service of God with a necessary dependence on the will of a mutable man, and religion of the good pleasure of the king, as if he were some God on earth, they doubtless little value the testimony of Holy Writ. But let them (at the least) yet learn of a heathen orator that in every public state, there are certain degrees of duty, for those who converse and live in it, by which may appear wherein the one are obliged to the other. Insomuch that the first part of this duty belongs to the immortal God, the second concerns the country, which is their common mother, the third, those who are of our blood, the other parts leading us step by step to our other neighbors. Now, although the crime of high treason be very heinous, yet according to the civilians, it always follows after sacrilege, an offence which properly pertains to the Lord God and His service, insomuch that they do confidently affirm that the robbing of a church is, by their rules, esteemed a greater crime than to conspire against the life of a prince.'

Thus much for this first question, wherein we persuade ourselves that any man may receive satisfaction if he be not utterly void of the fear of God.

THE SECOND QUESTION

Whether it be lawful to resist a prince who does infringe the law of
God, or ruin His Church: by whom, how, and how far it is lawful.

This question seems at the first view to be of a high and difficult nature, forsomuch as there being small occasion to speak
to princes that fear God. On the contrary, there will be much danger
to trouble the ears of those who acknowledge no other sovereign but
themselves, for which reason few or none have meddled with it, and if
any have at all touched it, it has been but as it were in passing by. The
question is, If it be lawful to resist a prince violating the law of God,
or ruinating the church, or hindering the restoring of it? If we hold
ourselves to the tenure of the Holy Scripture it will resolve us. For, if
in this case it had been lawful to the Jewish people (the which may
be easily gathered from the books of the Old Testament), yea, if it
had been enjoined them, I believe it will not be denied that the same
must be allowed to the whole people of any Christian kingdom or
country whatsoever. In the first place it must be considered that God
having chosen Israel from amongst all the nations of the earth to be
a peculiar people to Him, covenanted with them, that they should
be the people of God. This is written in divers places of Deuteronomy: the substance and tenor of this alliance was that all should be

careful in their several lines, tribes, and families in the land of Canaan, to serve God purely, who would have a church established amongst them forever, which may be drawn from the testimony of divers places, namely, that which is contained in the twenty-seventh chapter of Deuteronomy; there Moses and the Levites covenanting as in the name of God assembled all the people and said unto them: "This day, O Israel, art you become the people of God, obey you therefore His voice," etc (27:9). And Moses said, "When you hast passed the River of Jordan, you shall set six tribes on the mountain of Gerizim on the one side, and the six others on the mountain of Ebal, and then the Levites shall read the law of God, promising the observers all felicity, and threatening woe and destruction to the breakers thereof, and all the people shall answer, Amen" (Deut. 27:12-14ff), the which was afterwards performed by Joshua at his entering into the land of Canaan, and some few days before his death. We see by this that all the people is bound to maintain the law of God to perfect His church, and on the contrary to exterminate the idols of the land of Canaan, a covenant which can nowise appertain to particulars, but only to the whole body of the people, to which it also seems the encamping of all the tribes round about the ark of the Lord to have reference, to the end that all should look to the preservation of that which was committed to the custody of all.

Now for the use and practice of this covenant we may produce examples: the inhabitants of Gaba of the Tribe of Benjamin ravished the wife of a Levite, who died through their violence. The Levite divided his wife into twelve pieces and sent them to the twelve tribes, to the end that all the people together might wipe away so horrible a crime committed in Israel. All the people met together at Mizpah and required the Benjamites to deliver to be punished those who were culpable of this enormous crime, which they refused to perform. Wherefore with the allowance of God Himself, the states of the people with an universal consent renounced and made war against the

Benjamites, and by this means the authority of the second Table of the Law was maintained by the detriment and ruin of one entire tribe who had broken it in one of the precepts.

For the first we have an example sufficiently manifest in Joshua. After the Reubenites, Gadites, and Manassites were returned into their dwellings beyond Jordan, they incontinently built a goodly altar near unto the river; this seems contrary to the commandment of the Lord, who expressly forbids to sacrifice anywhere but in the land of Canaan only, where it was to be feared lest these men intended to serve idols. This business being communicated to the people inhabiting on this side Jordan, the place assigned for the meetings of the states was at Shiloh where the Ark of the Lord was. They all accordingly met and Phineas the High Priest, the son of Eleazar, was sent to the other to treat with them concerning this offense committed against the law. And to the end they might know all the people had a hand in this business, they sent also the principal men of every tribe to complain that the service of God is corrupted by this device, that God would be provoked by this rebellion and become an enemy, not only to the guilty, but also to all Israel, as heretofore in Baal-peor: briefly, that they should denounce open war against them, if they desisted not from this their manner of doing. There must of necessity have followed much mischief, if those tribes beyond Jordan had not protested that they erected that altar only for a memorial that the Israelites both on the one and the other side of Jordan both did and do profess one and the same religion, and at all times whensoever they have showed themselves negligent in the maintenance of the service of God, we have seen that they have ever been punished. This is the true cause wherefore they lost two battles against the Benjamites according as it appears in the end of the Book of Judges; for in so carefully undertaking to punish the rape and outrage done to a particular person, they clearly convinced themselves of much negligent profaneness in the maintenance of God's right by their continual negligence,

omission to punish both corporal and spiritual whoredoms; there was
then in these first times such a covenant between God and the people.

Now after that kings were given unto the people, there was so little purpose of disannulling or disbanding the former contract that
it was renewed and confirmed forever. We have formerly said at the
inaugurating of kings there was a double covenant treated of, to wit
"between God and the king"; and "between God and the people." The
agreement was first passed between "God, the king, and the people,"
or between the "high priest, the people" (which is named in the first
place in the twenty-third chapter of the second book of Chronicles)
"and the king." The intention of this was that the "people should be
the people of God" which is as much as to say that the people should
be the church of God. We have showed before to what end God contracted covenants with the king.

Let us now consider wherefore also He allies Himself with the
people. It is a most certain thing that God has not done this in vain,
and if the people had not "authority to promise, and to keep promise," it were vainly lost time to contract or covenant with them. It
may seem then that God has done like those creditors, which having
to deal with not very sufficient borrowers, take divers jointly bound
for one and the same sum, insomuch as two or more being bound
one for another and each of them apart, for the entire payment of
the total sum, he may demand his whole debt of which of them he
pleases. There was much danger to commit the custody of the church
to one man alone, and therefore God did recommend, and put it in
trust "to all the people." The king being raised to so slippery a place
might easily be corrupted. For fear lest the church should stumble
with him, God would have the people also to be respondents for it.
In the covenant of which we speak, God or (in His place) the High
Priest are stipulators, the king and all the people, to wit, Israel, do
jointly and voluntarily assume, promise, and oblige themselves for
one and the same thing. The High Priest demands if they promise

that the people shall be the people of God, that God shall always have His temple, His church amongst them, where He shall be purely served. The king is respondent; so also are the people (the whole body of the people representing, as it were, the office and place of one man) not severally, but jointly, as the words themselves make clear, being incontinent, and not by intermission or distance of time, the one after the other.

We see here then two undertakers, the king and Israel, who by consequence are bound one for another and each for the whole. For as when Caius and Titus have promised jointly to pay to their creditor Seius a certain sum, each of them is bound for himself and his companion, and the creditor may demand the sum of which of them he pleases. In the like manner the king for himself, and Israel for itself are bound with all circumspection to see that the church be not damnified: if either of them be negligent of their covenant, God may justly demand the whole of which of the two He pleases, and the more probably of the people than of the king, and for that many cannot so easily slip away as one, and have better means to discharge the debts than one alone. In like manner, as when two men that are indebted, especially to the public exchequer, the one is in such manner bound for the other that he can take no benefit of the division granted by the new constitutions of Justinian. So likewise the king and Israel, promising to pay tribute to God, who is the King of kings, for accomplishment whereof the one is obliged for the other. And as two covenanters by promise, especially in contracts, the obligation whereof exposes the obligees to forfeitures and hazards, such as this is here, the failings of the one endamages the other, so that if Israel forsake their God, and the king makes no account of it, he is justly guilty of Israel's delinquency. In like manner, if the king follow after strange gods and not content to be seduced himself, seek also to attract his subjects, endeavoring by all means to ruin the church, if Israel seek not to withdraw him from his rebellion, and contain him

within the limits of obedience, they make the fault of their king their
own transgression.

Briefly, as when there is danger that one of the debtors by con-
suming his goods may be disabled to give satisfaction, the other must
satisfy the creditors who ought not to be endamaged; though one of
his debtors have ill husbanded his estate, this ought not to be doubted
in regard of Israel toward their king, and of the king towards Israel in
case one of them apply himself to the service of idols, or break their
covenant in any other sort, the one of them must pay the forfeiture
and be punished for the other. Now that the covenant of which we at
this time treat is of this nature, it appears also by other testimonies of
Holy Scripture. Saul being established king of Israel, Samuel, priest
and prophet of the Lord, speaks in this manner to the people: "Both
you and your king which is over you serve the Lord your God, but if
you persevere in malice " (he taxes them of malice for that they preferred the government of a man before that of God) "you and your
king shall perish." He adds after the reason: "For it has pleased God
to choose you for His people" (1 Sam. 12:25, 22). You see here both
the parties evidently conjoined in the condition and the punishment.
In like manner Asa, king of Judah, by the council of the prophet Aza-
riah, assembles all the people at Jerusalem, to wit, Judah and Benjamin, to enter into covenant with God. Thither came also divers of the
tribes of Ephraim, Manasseh, and Simeon, who were come thither to
serve the Lord according to His own ordinance. After the sacrifices
were performed according to the law, the covenant was contracted in
these terms: "Whosoever shall not call upon the Lord God of Israel,
be he the least or the greatest, let him die the death" (2 Chron. 15:13).
In making mention of the greatest, you see that the king himself is
not excepted from the designed punishment.

But who may punish the king (for here is question of corporal
and temporal punishment) if it be not the whole body of the people
to whom the king swears and obliges himself, no more nor less than

the people do to the king? We read also that king Josiah, being of the age of twenty and five years, together with the whole people, makes a covenant with the Lord, the king and the people promising to keep the laws and ordinances of God, and even then for the better accomplishing of the tenure of this agreement, the idolatry of Baal was presently destroyed. If any will more exactly turn over the Holy Bible, he may well find other testimonies to this purpose.

But to what purpose should the consent of the people be required; wherefore should Israel or Judah be expressly bound to observe the law of God? For what reason should they promise so solemnly to be forever the people of God? If it be denied by the same reason that they had any authority from God, or power to free themselves from perjury, or to hinder the ruin of the church. For to what end should it serve to cause the people to promise to be the people of God, if they must and are bound to endure and suffer the king to draw them after strange gods. If the people be absolutely in bondage, wherefore is it commanded then, to take order that God be purely served? If it be so that they cannot properly oblige themselves to God, and if it be not lawful for them by all to endeavor the accomplishment of their promise, shall we say that God has made an agreement with them, which had no right neither to promise, nor to keep promise? But on the contrary, in this business of making a covenant with the people, God would openly and plainly show that the people have right to make, hold, and accomplish their promises and contracts. For, if he be not worthy to be heard in public court that will bargain or contract with a slave, or one that is under tutelage, shall it not be much more shameful to lay this imputation upon the Almighty, that He should contract with those who had no power to perform the conditions covenanted?

But for this occasion it was that when the kings had broken their covenants, the prophets always addressed themselves to the House of Judah and Jacob, and to Samaria, to advertise them of their duties. Furthermore, they required the people that they not only withdraw

themselves from sacrificing to Baal, but also that they call down his
idol, and destroy his priests and service, yea, even maugre the king
himself. For example, Ahab having killed the prophets of God, the
prophet Elijah assembles the people, and as it were convented the
estates, and does there tax, reprehend, and reprove every one of them;
the people at his exhortation take and put to death the priests of
Baal. And forsomuch as the king neglected his duty, it behooved Israel more carefully to discharge theirs without tumult, not rashly, but
by public authority, the estates being assembled and the equity of the
cause orderly debated, and sufficiently cleared before they came to the
execution of justice. On the contrary, so often and always when Israel
has failed to oppose their king, which would overthrow the service
of God, that which has been formerly said of the two debtors, the
inability and ill husbandry of the one does ever prejudice the other,
the same happened to them; for as the king has been punished for his
idolatry and disloyalty, the people have also been chastised for their
negligence, connivance, and stupidity, and it has commonly happened
that the kings have been much more often swayed and drawn others
with them than the people, forsomuch as ordinarily the great ones
mold themselves into the fashion of the king, and the people conform
themselves in humors to those who govern them; to be brief, all more
usually offend after the example of one than that one will reform
himself as he sees all the rest.

This which we say will, perhaps, appear more plainly by examples.
What do we suppose to have been the cause of the defeat and overthrow of the army of Israel with their king Saul? Does God correct
the people for the sins of the prince? Is the child beaten instead of
the father? It is a discourse not easily to be digested, say the civilians,
to maintain that the children should bear the punishments due for
the offenses of their fathers; the laws do not permit that anyone shall
suffer for the wickedness of another. "Now God forbid that the judge
of all the world," said Abraham, "should destroy the innocent with

the guilty" (Gen. 18:25). "On the contrary," says the Lord, "as the life of the father, so the life of the son is in my hands; the fathers shall not be put to death for the children, neither shall the children be put to death for the fathers; every man shall be put to death for his own sin" (Deut. 24:16). That overthrow, then, did it not proceed because the people opposed not Saul when he violated the law of God, but applauded that miserable prince when he wickedly persecuted the best men, as David and the priests of the Lord?

Amongst many other examples let us only produce some few. The same Saul to enlarge the possessions of the tribe of Judah broke the public faith granted to the Gibeonites, at the first entry of the people into the land of Canaan, and put to death as many of the Gibeonites as he could come by. By this execution Saul broke the third commandment, for God had been called to witness this agreement, and the sixth also, insomuch as he murdered the innocent; he ought to have maintained the authority of the two Tables of the Law, and thereupon it is said that Saul and his house have committed this wickedness. In the meantime, after the death of Saul, and David being established king, the Lord being demanded made answer that it was already the third year that the whole country of Israel was afflicted with famine because of this cruelty, and the hand of the Lord ceased not to strike until seven men of the house of Saul were given to the Gibeonites, who put them to death, seeing that everyone ought to bear his own burden, and that no man is esteemed the inheritor of another's crime; wherefore they say that all the whole people of Israel deserved to be punished for Saul, who was already dead, and had (as it might seem) that controversy buried in the same grave with him, but only in regard that the people neglected to oppose a mischief so public and apparent, although they ought and might have done it. Think you it reason that any should be punished unless they deserve it? And in what have the people here failed but in suffering the offense of their king.

In like manner when David commanded Joab and the governors of Israel to number the people, he is taxed to have committed a great fault; for even as Israel provoked the anger of God in demanding a king, one in whose wisdom they seemed to repose their safety, even so David did much forget himself in hoping for victory through the multitude of his subjects; forsomuch as that is properly (according to the saying of the prophet) to sacrifice unto their net, and burn incense unto their drag, a kind of abominable idolatry; for the governors, they seeing that it would draw evil on the people, drew back a little at the first; afterwards, as it were, to be rid of the importunity they made the enrollment; in the mean season all the people are punished, and not David alone, but also the ancients of Israel, who represented the whole body of the people, put on sack-cloth and ashes, the which, notwithstanding, was not done nor practiced when David committed those horrible sins of murder and adultery. Who sees not in this last act that all had sinned, and that all should repent; and finally that all were chastised, to wit, David, who had provoked God by so wicked a commandment, the governors (as peers and assessors of the kingdom, ought in the name of all Israel to have opposed the king) by their connivance and over-weak resistance, and all the people also who made their appearance to be enrolled? God, in this respect, did like a chief commander or general of an army; he chastised the offense of the whole camp by a sudden alarm given to all, and by the exemplary punishments of some particulars to keep all the rest in better awe and order.

But tell me wherefore after that the King Manasseh had polluted the Temple at Jerusalem, do we read that God not only taxed Manasseh, but all the people also? Was it not to advertise Israel, one of the sureties, that if they keep not the king within the limits of his duty, they should all smart for it; for what meant the prophet Jeremiah to say that the house of Judah is in subjection to the Assyrians, because of the impiety and cruelty of Manasseh, but because they were guilty of all his offenses, because they made no resistance?

Wherefore Saint Augustine and Saint Ambrose said Herod and Pilate condemned Jesus Christ, the priests delivered Him to be crucified, the people seem to have some compassion; notwithstanding all are punished. And wherefore so? Forsomuch as they are all guilty of His death, in that they did not deliver Him out of the hands of those wicked judges and governors. There must also be added to this many other proofs drawn from divers authors for the further explication of this point, were it not that the testimonies of holy scripture ought to suffice Christians.

Furthermore, insomuch as it is the duty of a good magistrate rather to endeavor to hinder and prevent a mischief than to chastise the delinquents after the offense is committed, as good physicians who prescribe a diet to allay and prevent diseases, as well as medicines to cure them; in like manner a people truly affected to true religion will not simply consent themselves to reprove and repress a prince who would abolish the law of God, but also will have special regard that through malice and wickedness he innovate nothing that may hurt the same, or that in tract of time may corrupt the pure service of God; and instead of supporting public offenses committed against the Divine Majesty, they will take away all occasions wherewith the offenders might cover their faults; we read that to have been practiced by all Israel by a decree of Parliament in the assembly of the whole people, to remonstrate to those beyond Jordan, touching the altar they had built, and by the king Hezekiah, who caused the brazen serpent to be broken.

It is then lawful for Israel to resist the king who would overthrow the law of God and abolish His church; and not only so, but also they ought to know that in neglecting to perform this duty, they make themselves culpable of the same crime, and shall bear the like punishment with their king.

If their assaults be verbal, their defense must be likewise verbal; if the sword be drawn against them, they may also take arms and fight either with tongue or hand, as occasion is. Yea, if they be assailed by surprisals, they may make use both of ambuscades and countermines, there being no rule in lawful war that directs them for the manner, whether it be by open assailing their enemy or by close surprising; provided always that they carefully distinguish between advantageous stratagems and perfidious treason, which is always unlawful.

But I see well, here will be an objection made. What will you say? That a whole people, that beast of many heads, must they run in a mutinous disorder to order the business of the commonwealth? What address or direction is there in an unruly and unbridled multitude? What counsel or wisdom, to manage the affairs of state?

When we speak of all the people, we understand by that only those who hold their authority from the people, to wit, the magistrates, who are inferior to the king and whom the people have substituted or established, as it were, consorts in the empire, and with a kind of tribunitial authority to restrain the encroachments of sovereignty, and to represent the whole body of the people. We understand also the assembly of the estates, which is nothing else but an epitome or brief collection of the kingdom, to whom all public affairs have special and absolute reference; such were the seventy ancients in the kingdom of Israel, amongst whom the high priest was, as it were, president, and they judged all matters of greatest importance, those seventy being first chosen by six out of each tribe which came out of the land of Egypt, then the heads or governors of provinces. In like manner the judges and provosts of towns, the captains of thousands, the centurions and others who commanded over families, the most valiant, noble, and otherwise notable personages, of whom was composed the body of the states, assembled divers times as it plainly appears by the word of the holy scripture. At the election of the first king, who was Saul, all the ancients of Israel assembled together at Kama. In like manner all Israel was assembled, or all Judah and Benjamin, etc. Now, it is no way probable that all the people, one by one, met together there. Of this rank there are in every well-governed kingdom the princes, the officers of the crown, the peers, the greatest and most notable lords, the deputies of provinces, of whom the ordinary body of the estate is composed, or the parliament or the diet, or other assembly, according to the different names used in divers countries of the world; in which assemblies, the principal care is had both for the preventing and reforming either of disorder or detriment in church or commonwealth.

For as the councils of Basil and Constance have decreed (and well decreed) that the universal council is in authority above the bishop of Rome, so in like manner, the whole chapter may overrule the bishop, the university the rector, the court the president. Briefly, he, whosoever he is who has received authority from a company, is inferior to that whole company, although he be superior to any of the particular members of it. Also is it without any scruple or doubt that Israel, who demanded and established a king as governor of the public, must needs be above Saul, established at their request and for Israel's sake, as it shall be more fully proved hereafter. And forsomuch as an orderly proceeding is necessarily required in all affairs discreetly addressed, and that it is not so probably hopeful that order shall be observed amongst so great a number of people, yea, and that there oftentimes occur occasions which may not be communicated to a multitude without manifest danger of the commonwealth, we say, that all that which has been spoken of privileges granted and right committed to the people ought to be referred to the officers and deputies of the kingdom, and all that which has been said of Israel is to be understood of the princes and elders of Israel, to whom these things were granted and committed as the practice also has verified.

The queen Athaliah, after the death of her son Ahaziah king of Judah, put to death all those of the royal blood except little Joash, who, being yet in the cradle, was preserved by the piety and wisdom of his aunt Jehoshebah. Athaliah possesses herself of the government, and reigned six years over Judah. It may well be the people murmured between their teeth, and dared not by reason of danger express what they thought in their minds.

Finally, Jehoiada, the high priest, the husband of Jehoshebah, having secretly made a league and combination with the chief men of the kingdom, did anoint and crown king his nephew Joash, being but seven years old. And he did not content himself to drive the queen mother from the royal throne, but he also put her to death, and presently overthrew the idolatry of Baal. This deed of Jehoiada is approved, and by good reason, for he took on him the defense of a good cause, for he assailed the tyranny, and not the kingdom. The tyranny, I say, which had no title, as our modern civilians speak. For by no law were women admitted to the government of the kingdom of Judah. Furthermore, that tyranny was in vigor and practice, for Athaliah had with unbounded mischief and cruelty invaded the realm of her nephews, and in the administration of that government committed infinite wickedness, and what was the worst of all, had cast off the service of the living God to adore and compel others with her to worship the idol of Baal. Therefore then was she justly punished, and by him who had a lawful calling and authority to do it. For Jehoiada was not a private and particular person, but the high priest, to whom the knowledge of civil causes did then belong. And besides, he had for his associates, the principal men of the kingdom, the Levites, and being himself the king's kinsman and ally. Now forsomuch as he assembled not the estates at Mizpah, according to the accustomed manner, he is not reproved for it, neither for that he consulted and contrived the matter secretly, for that if he had held any other manner of proceeding, the business must probably have failed in the execution and success.

A combination or conjuration is good or ill, according as the end whereunto it is addressed is good or ill, and perhaps also according as they are affected who are the managers of it. We say then, that the princes of Judah have done well, and that in following any other course they had failed of the right way. For even as the guardian ought to take charge and care that the goods of his pupil fall not into loss and detriment, and if he omit his duty therein, he may be compelled to give an account thereof, in like manner, those to whose custody and tuition the people have committed themselves, and whom they have constituted their tutors and defenders ought to maintain them safe and entire in all their rights and privileges. To be short, as it is lawful for a whole people to resist and oppose tyranny, so likewise the principal persons of the kingdom may as heads, and for the good of the whole body, confederate and associate themselves together, and as in a public state, that which is done by the greatest part is esteemed and taken as the act of all, so in like manner must it be said to be done, which the better part of the most principal have acted, briefly, that all the people had their hand in it.

But here presents itself another question, the which deserves to be considered and amply debated in regard of the circumstance of time. Let us put the case that a king seeking to abolish the law of God, or ruin the church, that all the people or the greatest part yield their consent, that all the princes or the greatest number of them make no reckoning, and notwithstanding, a small handful of people, to wit, some of the princes and magistrates desire to preserve the law of God entirely and inviolably and to serve the Lord purely, what may it be lawful for them to do if the king seek to compel those men to be idolaters, or will take from them the exercise of true religion? We speak not here of private and particular persons considered one by one, and who in that manner are not held as parts of the entire body, as the planks, the nails, the pegs are no part of the ship, neither the stones, the rafters, nor the rubbish are any part of the house. But we speak of some town or province, which makes a portion of a kingdom, as the prow, the poop, the keel, and other parts make a ship; the foundation, the roof, and the walls make a house. We speak also of the magistrate who governs such a city or province.

If we must make our defense with producing of examples, although we have not many ready by reason of the backwardness and carelessness of men when there is question to maintain the service of God, notwithstanding, we have some few to be examined and received according as they deserve. Libna, a town of the priests withdrew itself from the obedience of Joram, king of Judah, and left that prince, because he had abandoned the God of his fathers, whom those of the town would serve, and it may be they feared also lest in the end they should be compelled to sacrifice to Baal. In like manner when that the king Antiochus commanded that all the Jews should embrace his religion and should forsake that which the God Almighty had taught them, Mattathias answered, "We will not obey, nor will we do anything contrary to our religion." Neither did he only speak, but also, being transported with the zeal of Phineas, he killed with his own hands a Jew who constrained his fellow citizens to sacrifice to idols. Then he took arms and retired into the mountain, gathered troops, and made war against Antiochus for religion and for his country, with such success that he regained Jerusalem, broke and brought to nothing the power of the pagans whom they had gathered to ruin the church, and then re-established the pure service of God. If we will know who this Mattathias was, he was the father of the Maccabees of the tribe of Levi, insomuch as it was not lawful for him, according to the received custom and right of his race to restore the kingdom by arms from the tyranny of Antiochus. His followers were such as fled to the mountains together with the inhabitants of Modin, to whom had adjoined themselves divers neighboring Jews and other fugitives from sundry quarters of Judea; all who solicitously desired the re-establishment of the church. Almost all the rest, yea, the principals, obeyed Antiochus, and that after the rout of his army and his own miserable death. Although there was then a fair occasion to shake off his yoke, yet the Jews sought to the son of Antiochus, and entreated him to take on him the kingdom, promising him fidelity and obedience.

I might here produce the example of Deborah. The Lord God had subjected Israel to Jabin king of Canaan, and they had remained in this servitude the space of twenty years, who might seem in some sort to have gained a right by prescription over the kingdom, and together also, that almost all Israel followed after strange gods. The principal and most powerful tribes, to wit, Reuben, Ephraim, Benjamin, Dan, Asher, and some others, adhered wholly to Jabin. Yet notwithstanding, the prophetess Deborah who judged Israel caused the tribes of Zebulon, Naphtali, and Issachar, or at the least some of all those tribes, to take arms under the conduct of Barak, and they overthrew Sisera the lieutenant of Jabin, and delivered Israel, who had no thought of liberty and was content to remain in bondage, and having shaken off the yoke of the Canaanites they re established the pure service of the living God. But forsomuch as Deborah seems to have an extraordinary vocation, and that the scripture does not approve in express terms the doings of them of Libna, although that in not disallowing of their proceedings it may seem in some sort to allow them, and for that the history of the Maccabees has had no great authority in the ancient church, and for that it is commonly held that an assertion must be proved by laws and testimonies, not by examples, let us examine by the effect what we ought to judge according to the right of the matter now in question.

We have formerly said that the king did swear to keep the law of God, and promised to the uttermost of his power to maintain the church; that the people of Israel considered in one body, covenanting by the high priest, made the same promise to God. Now, at this present, we say that all the towns and all the magistrates of these towns, which are parts and portions of the kingdom, promise each of them on his own behalf, and in express terms, the which all towns and Christian communalties have also done, although it has been but with a tacit consent. Joshua, being very old and near to his death, assembled all Israel at Shechem in the presence of God, to wit, before the ark of the covenant which was there. It is said that the ancients of the people, the heads of the tribe, the judges and governors, and all who had any public command in the town of Israel met together there, where they swore to observe and keep the law of the Lord, and did willingly put on the yoke of the Almighty God; whereby it appears that these magistrates did oblige themselves in the names of their towns and communalties, who did send them to take order, that God should be served throughout the whole country, according as He had revealed in His law. And Joshua, for his part, having passed this contract of agreement between God and the people, and enregistered the whole, according as it was done, for a perpetual memorial of the matter he incontinently set up a stone.

If there were occasion to remove the ark of the Lord, the principals of the country and towns, the captains, the centurions, the provosts, and others were summoned by the decree and commandment of David, and of the synagogue of Israel, if there be a purpose of building the Lord's temple, the same course is observed. And to the end it be not supposed that some alteration has been inserted after the creation of kings. In the times of Joash and Josiah, when there was question of renewing the covenant between God and the people, all the estates met together, and all were bound and obliged particularly. Also not only the king, but the kingdom, and not only all the kingdom, but also all the pastors of the kingdom, promise each of them for themselves, fidelity and obedience to God. I say again that not only the king and the people, but also all the towns of Israel and their magistrates oblige themselves to God, and, as homagers to their liege lord, tie themselves to be His forever, with and against all men. For further proof of the aforesaid, I would entreat the reader diligently to turn over the Holy Bible, especially in the books of the Kings and the Chronicles. But for a yet more ample explication of this matter, let us produce for example what is in practice at this day.

In the empire of Germany, when the emperor is to be crowned, the electors and princes of the empire, as well secular as ecclesiastical, meet together personally, or else send their ambassadors. The prelates, earls and barons, and all the deputies of the imperial towns come thither also, or else send special proxies; then do they their homage to the emperor, either for themselves or for those whom they represent, with and under certain conditions. Now, let us presuppose that one of these who has done homage voluntarily, afterwards endeavors to depose the emperor, and advance himself into his place, and that the princes and barons deny their sovereign the succor and tribute which they owe him, and that they have intelligence with that other who conspired and sought to possess himself of the imperial throne. Think you that they of Strasbourg or of Nuremberg, who have bound themselves by faith unto the lawful emperor, have not lawful right to repress and exclude this traitorous intruder? Yea on the contrary, if they do it not, if they give not succor to the emperor in this his necessity, think you that they have satisfied or performed their fealty and promise, seeing that he who has not preserved his governor when he had means to do it ought to be held as culpable and guilty as he who offered the violence and injury unto him? If it be so (as every one may sufficiently see it is) is it not then lawful for the men of Libna and of Modin? And does not their duty enjoin them to do as much as if the other estates of the kingdom have left God, to whose service and pleasure they know and acknowledge themselves to be bound to render obedience?

Let us imagine then some Joram or Antiochus who abolishes true religion and lifts up himself above God, that Israel connives and is content, what should that town do which desires to serve God purely? First, they should say with Joshua, for their parts, look whom you desire rather to obey, the living God, or the gods of the Amorites; for our parts, we and our families will serve the Lord. Choose you then, I say, if you will obey in this point him who without any right

usurps that power and authority which no way appertains unto him;
for my part, happen what may, I will keep my faith to him to whom I
promised it. I make no question but that Joshua would have done the
uttermost of his endeavor to maintain the pure service of the living
God in Timnathserah, a town of Ephraim, where his house and estate
lay, if the Israelites besides had so much forgotten themselves as to
have worshiped the god of the Amorites in the land of Canaan.

But if the king should pass yet further, and send his lieutenants to
compel us to become idolaters, and if he commands us to drive God
and His service from amongst us, shall we not rather shut our gates
against the king and his officers than drive out of our town the Lord
who is the King of kings? Let the burgesses and citizens of towns,
let the magistrates and governors of the people of God dwelling in
towns, consider with themselves that they have contracted two covenants and taken two oaths. The first and most ancient with God, to
whom the people have sworn to be His people; the second and next
following, with the king, to whom the people have promised obedience, as unto him who is the governor and conductor of the people
of God. So then, as if a viceroy conspiring against his sovereign, although he had received from him an unlimited authority, if he should
summon us to deliver the king whom he held besieged within the
enclosure of our walls, we ought not to obey him, but resist with the
uttermost of our power and means, according to the tenor of our oath
of allegiance. In like manner think we, that it is not a wickedness of
all most detestable, if at the pleasure of a prince who is the vassal and
servant of God, we should drive God from dwelling amongst us, or
deliver Him (as far as in us lies) into the hands of His enemies.

You will say, it may be that the towns appertain to the prince. And
I answer that the towns consist not of a heap of stones, but of that
which we call people, that the people is the people of God, to whom
they are first bound by oath, and secondly to the king. For the towns,
although that the kings have power over them, notwithstanding the

right of inheritance of the soil belongs to the citizens and owners, for all that which is in a kingdom is indeed under the dominion of the king, but not of his proper patrimony. God in truth is the only Lord proprietor of all things, and it is of Him that the king holds his royalties and the people their patrimony. This is as much as to say, you will reply, that for the cause of religion it shall be lawful for the subjects to revolt from the obedience of their king. If this be once granted, it will presently open a gap to rebellion? But, harken, I pray you patiently, and consider this matter more thoroughly. I might answer in a word that of two things, if the one must needs be done, it were much better to forsake the king than God; or with Saint Augustine in his fourth book concerning the city of God, chapter four, and in the nineteenth book, and chapter twenty-one, that where there is no justice, there is no commonwealth; that there is no justice when he that is a mortal man would pull another man out of the hands of the immortal God, to make him a slave of the devil, seeing that justice is a virtue that gives to everyone that which is his own, and that those who draw their necks out of the yoke of such rulers, deliver themselves from the tyranny of wicked spirits and abandon a multitude of robbers, and not the commonwealth.

But to re-assume this discourse a little higher, those who shall carry themselves as has been formerly said, seem in no way accusable of the crime of revolt. Those are said properly to quit the king or the commonwealth, which, with the heart and purpose of an enemy, withdraw themselves from the obedience of the king or the commonwealth, by means whereof they are justly accounted adversaries and are oftentimes much more to be feared than any other enemies. But those of whom we now speak do nothing resemble them. First, they do in no sort refuse to obey, provided that they be commanded that which they may lawfully do, and that it be not against the honor of God.

They pay willingly the taxes, customs, imposts, and ordinary payments, provided that with these they seek not to abolish the tribute which they owe unto God. They obey Caesar while he commands in the quality of Caesar; but when Caesar passes his bounds, when he usurps that dominion which is none of his own, when he endeavors to assail the Throne of God, when he wars against the Sovereign Lord, both of himself and the people, they then esteem it reasonable not to obey Caesar, and yet after this, to speak properly, they do no acts of hostility. He is properly an enemy who stirs up, who provokes another, who out of military insolence prepares and sets forth parties to war. They have been urged and assailed by open war, and close and treacherous surprisals; when death and destruction environ them round about, then they take arms and wait their enemies' assaults. You cannot have peace with your enemies when you will, for if you lay down your weapons, if you give over making war, they will not for all that disarm themselves and lose their advantage. But for these men, desire but peace and you have it; give over but assailing them, and they will lay down their arms; cease to fight against God, and they will presently leave the lists. Will you take their swords out of their hands? Abstain you only then from striking, seeing they are not the assailants, but the defendants; sheathe your sword, and they will presently cast their buckler on the ground, which has been the reason that they have been often surprised by perfidious ambuscades, whereof these our times have afforded over-frequent examples.

Now, as we cannot call that servant stubborn or a fugitive, who puts by the blow which his lord strikes at him with his sword, or who withdraws or hides himself from his master's fury, or shuts his chamber door upon him until his choler and heat be passed over, much less ought we to esteem those seditious who (holding the name and place of servants and subjects) shut the gates of a city against their prince, transported with anger, being ready to do all his just commandments after he has recovered his judgment and related his former indignation. We must place in this rank, David, commander of the army of

Israel, under Saul, a furious king. David, oppressed with calumnies and false taxations, watched and waylaid from all parts he retired unto, defended himself in unaccessible mountains and provided for his defense to oppose the walls of Ceila against the fury of the king; yea, he drew unto his party all those that he could, not to take away Saul's life from him, as it plainly appeared afterwards, but to defend his own cause. See wherefore Jonathan, the son of Saul, made no difficulty to make alliance with David and to renew it from time to time, the which is called the alliance of the Almighty. And Abigail says in express words that David was wrongfully assailed, and that he made the war of God.

We must also place in this rank the Maccabees, who having good means to maintain wars were content to receive peace from king Demetrius and others, which Antiochus had offered them before, because by it, they should be secured in the free possession and exercise of their religion. We may remember that those who in our times have fought for true religion against Antichrist, both in Germany and France, have laid down arms as soon as it was permitted them to serve God truly according to His ordinance, and oftentimes having fair means and occasion to advance and continue the war to their much advantage, as when the Philistines compelled Saul to cease attack and Antioch to desist from an assault upon its neighbors, and other occasions when everything favored further warfare. See then the marks which distinguish and separate sufficiently those of whom we speak from rebels or seditious.

But let us yet see other evident testimonies of the equity of their cause; for their defection is of that nature that, take away but the occasion, if some extreme necessity compel not the contrary, they presently return to their former condition, and then you cannot properly say they separated themselves from the king or the commonalty, but that they left Joram and Antiochus, or if you will, the tyranny and unlawful power of one alone, or of divers particulars who had no authority nor right to exact obedience in the same manner as they commanded. The doctors of the Sorbonne have taught us the like sundry times, whereof we will allege some examples.

About the year 1300 Pope Boniface VIII, seeking to appropriate to his See the royalties that belonged to the crown of France, Philip the Fair, the then king, did taunt him somewhat sharply: the tenor of whose tart letters are these:

"Philip by the Grace of God, King of the French, to Boniface, calling himself Sovereign Bishop, little or no health at all. Be it known to the great foolishness and unbounded rashness that in temporal matters we have only God for our superior, and that the vacancy of certain churches belongs to us by royal prerogative, and that appertains to us only to gather the fruits, and we will defend the possession thereof against all opposers with the edge of our swords, accounting them fools and without brains who hold a contrary opinion."

In those times all men acknowledged the pope for God's vicar on earth, and head of the universal church, insomuch that (as it is said) common error went instead of a law, notwithstanding the Sorbonists being assembled and demanded, made answer that the king and the kingdom might safely without blame or danger of schism exempt themselves from his obedience and flatly refuse that which the pope demanded; forsomuch as it is not the separation but the cause which makes the schism, and if there were schism, it should be only in separating from Boniface, and not from the church, nor from the pope, and that there was no danger nor offence in so remaining until some honest man were chosen pope. Everyone knows into what perplexities the consciences of a whole kingdom would fall which held themselves separated from the church, if this distinction be not true. I would demand now, if it be not yet more lawful to make use of this distinction, when a king invades and encroaches on the jurisdiction of God, and oppresses with hard servitude, the souls dearly bought with the precious blood of Jesus Christ. Let us add another example.

In the year of our Lord 1408, when pope Benedict XIII did oppose the French church by tributes and exactions, the clergy, assembled by the command of King Charles VI decreed that the king and inhabitants of the kingdom ought not to obey Benedict, who was a heretic, a schismatic, and altogether unworthy of that dignity, the which the estates of the kingdom approved, and the parliament of Paris confirmed by a decree. The same clergy also ordained that those who had been excommunicated by that pope, as forsakers and enemies of the church, should be presently absolved, nullifying all such excommunications, and this has been practiced not in France only, but in other places also, as histories do credibly report, the which gives us just occasion most perspicuously to see and know that if he who holds the place of a prince do govern ill, there may be a separation from him without incurring justly the blame of revolt; for that they are things in themselves directly contrary, to leave a bad pope and forsake the church, a wicked king, and the kingdom. To return to those of Lobna, they seem to have followed this before remembered expedient; for after the re-establishment of the service of God they presently became again the subjects of king Hezekiah. And if this distinction be allowed place, when a pope encroaches on the rights of any prince, which notwithstanding in some cases acknowledges him for his sovereign, is it not much more allowable if a prince, who is a vassal in that respect, endeavors to assure and appropriate to himself the rights of God? Let us conclude then, to end this discourse, that all the people by the authority of those into whose hands they have committed their power, or divers of them, may and ought to reprove and repress a prince who commands things against God. In like manner, that all, or at the least, the principals of provinces or towns, under the authority of the chief magistrates, established first by God, and secondly by the prince, may according to law and reason hinder the entrance of idolatry within the enclosure of their walls and maintain their true religion, yea, further, they may extend the confines of the church, which is but one, and in failing hereof, if they have means to do it, they justly incur the penalty of high treason against the Divine Majesty.

I. WHETHER PRIVATE MEN MAY RESIST BY ARMS

It remains now that we speak of particulars who are private persons. First, particulars or private persons are not bound to take up arms against the prince who would compel them to become idolaters. The covenant between God and all the people who promise to be the people of God does not in any sort bind them to that; for as that which belongs to the whole universal body is in no sort proper to particulars, so in like manner that which the body owes and is bound to perform cannot by any sensible reason be required of particular persons; neither does their duty anything oblige them to it, for everyone is bound to serve God in that proper vocation to which he is called. Now private persons, they have no power; they have no public command, nor any calling to unsheathe the sword of authority, and therefore as God has not put the sword into the hands of private men, so does He not require in any sort that they should strike with it. It is said to them, "put up thy sword into thy scabbard" (John 18:11). On the contrary the apostles say of magistrates, "they carry not the sword in vain" (Rom. 13:4). If particular men draw it forth they make themselves delinquents. If magistrates be slow and negligent to use it when just occasion is offered, they are likewise justly blamable of negligence in performing their duties, and equally guilty with the former.

But you will say unto me, has not God made a covenant, as well with particular persons as with the generality, with the least as well as the highest? To what purpose was circumcision and baptism ordained? What means that frequent repetition of the covenant in so many passages of holy writ? All this is true, but the consideration hereof is diverse in their several kinds. For as all the subjects of a good and faithful prince, of what degree soever they be, are bound to obey him, but some of them, notwithstanding, have their particular duty, as magistrates must hold others in obedience; in like manner all men are bound to serve God, but some are placed in a higher rank, have received greater authority, in so much as they are account able for the offenses of others, if they attend not the charges of the commonalty carefully.

The kings, the commonalties of the people, the magistrates into whose hands the whole body of the commonwealth has committed the sword of authority, must and ought to take care that the church be maintained and preserved; particulars ought only to look that they render themselves members of this church. Kings and popular estates are bound to hinder the pollution or ruin of the temple of God and ought to free and defend it from all corruption within and all injury from without. Private men must take order that their bodies, the temples of God, be pure, that they may be fit receptacles for the Holy Ghost to dwell in them. "If any man defile the temple of God," saith the apostle, "him shall God destroy; for the temple of God is holy, which temple ye are" (1 Cor. 3:17); to the former He gives the sword which they bear with authority; to the other He recommends the sword of the Spirit only, to wit, the word of God, wherewith Saint Paul arms all Christians against the assaults of the devil. What shall then private men do, if the king will constrain them to serve idols? If the magistrates into whose hands the people have consigned their authority, or if the magistrates of the place, where these particulars dwell, do oppose these proceedings of the king, let them in God's name obey their leaders and employ all their means (as in the service of God) to aid the holy and commendable enterprises of those who oppose themselves lawfully against his wicked intention. Amongst others they have the examples of the centurions and men at arms, who readily and cheerfully obeyed the princes of Judah, who stirred up by Jehoiada purged the church from all profanation and delivered the kingdom from the tyranny of Athaliah. But if the princes and magistrates approve the course of an outrageous and irreligious prince, or if they do not resist him, we must lend our ears to the counsel of Jesus Christ, to wit, retire ourselves into some other place. We have the example of the faithful mixed among the ten tribes of Israel, who, seeing the true service of God abolished by Jeroboam, and that none made any account of it, they retired themselves into the territories of Judah, where religion remained in her purity. Let us rather forsake our livelihoods and lives than God, let us rather be crucified ourselves, than crucify the Lord of Life: "fear not them," says the Lord, "who can only kill the body" (Matt. 10:28). He Himself, His apostles, and an infinite number of Christian martyrs have taught us this by their examples; shall it not then be permitted to any private person to resist by arms? What shall we say of Moses, who led Israel away in despite of King Pharaoh? And of Ehud, who after ten years' servitude, when Israel might seem to belong by right of prescription to him who held the possession thereof, killed Eglon, the king of Moab, and delivered Israel from the yoke of the Moabites, and of Jehu, who put to death his lord the king Joram, extirpated the race of Ahab, and destroyed the priests of Baal. Were not these particulars? I answer that if they be considered in themselves, they may well be accounted particular persons, insomuch as they had not any ordinary vocation. But seeing that we know that they were called extraordinarily, and that God Himself has (if we may so speak) put His sword into their hands, be it far from us to account them particular or private persons, but rather let us esteem them by many degrees, excelling any ordinary magistrates whatsoever.

The calling of Moses is approved by the express word of God, and by most evident miracles: it is said of Ehud that God stirred him up to kill the tyrant and deliver Israel: for Jehu, he was anointed by the commandment of the prophet Elisha to root out the race of Ahab, besides that the principal men saluted him king before he executed anything. There may as much be said of all the rest, whose examples are propounded in holy writ. But where God Almighty does not speak with His own mouth, nor extraordinarily by His prophets, it is there that we ought to be exceedingly cautious and to stand upon our guard; for if any, supposing he is inspired by the Holy Ghost, do attribute to himself the before-mentioned authority, I would entreat him to look that he be not puffed up with vainglory, and lest he make not a God to himself of his own fancy and sacrifice to his own inventions. Let him not then be conceived with vanity, lest instead of fruit he bring forth deluding lies. Let the people also be advised on their parts, lest in desiring to fight under the banner of Jesus Christ they run not to their own confusion to follow the army of some Galilean Theudas, or of Bar Kokhba; as it happened to the peasants and Anabaptists of Munster in Germany. I will not say, notwithstanding, that the same God who to punish our offenses has sent us in these our days both Pharaohs and Ahabs, may not sometimes raise up extraordinary deliverances to His people: certainly His justice and His mercy continue to all ages, firm and immutable.

Now, if these visible miracles appear not as in former times, we may yet at the least fall by the effects that God works miraculously in our hearts, which is when we have our minds free from all ambition, a true and earnest zeal, a right knowledge, and conscience, lest being guided by the spirit of error or ambition, we rather make idols of our own imaginations than serve and worship the true and living God.

II. WHETHER IT BE LAWFUL TO TAKE ARMS FOR RELIGION

Furthermore, to take away all scruple, we must necessarily answer those who esteem, or else would that others should think they hold that opinion, that the church ought not to be defended by arms. They say withal that it was not without a great mystery that God did forbid in the law that the altar should be made or adorned with the help of any tool of iron; in like manner at the building of the temple of Solomon, there was not heard any noise of ax or hammer or other tools of iron, from whence they collect the church which is the lively temple of the Lord ought not to be reformed by arms, yea, as if the stones of the altar and of the temple were hewed and taken out of the quarries without any instrument of iron, which the text of the holy scripture does sufficiently clear.

But if we oppose to this goodly allegory that which is written in the fourth chapter of the Book of Nehemiah, that one part of the people carried mortar and another part stood ready with their weapons, that some held in one hand their swords and with the other carried the materials to the workmen, for the rebuilding of the temple; to the end, by this means, to prevent their enemies from ruining their work; we say also that the church is neither advanced nor edified by these material weapons, but by these arms it is warranted and preserved from the violence of the enemies, which will not by any means endure the increase of it. Briefly, there has been an infinite number of good kings and princes (as histories do testify) which by arms have maintained and defended the service of God against pagans. They reply readily to this that wars in this manner were allowable under the law; but since the time that grace has been offered by Jesus Christ, who would not enter into Jerusalem mounted on a brave horse, but meekly sitting on an ass, this manner of proceeding has had an end. I answer first that all agree with me in this: that our Savior Christ, during all the time that He conversed in this world took not on Him the office of a judge or king, but rather of a private person, and a delinquent by imputation of our transgressions, so that it is an allegation besides the purpose to say that He hath not managed arms.

But I would willingly demand of such exceptionalists whether that they think by the coming of Jesus Christ in the flesh that magistrates have lost their right in the sword of authority? If they say so, Saint Paul contradicts them, who says that the magistrates carry not the sword in vain, and did not refuse their assistance and power against the violence of those who had conspired his death. And if they consent to the saying of the apostle, to what purpose should the magistrates bear the sword if it be not to serve God, who has committed it to them, to defend the good and punish the bad? Can they do better service than to preserve the church from the violence of the wicked, and to deliver the flock of Christ from the swords of murderers? I would demand of them, yet, whether they think that all use of arms is forbidden to Christians? If this be their opinion, then would I know of them wherefore Christ did grant to the centurion his request? Wherefore did He give so excellent a testimony of him? Wherefore does Saint John the Baptist command the men at arms to content themselves with their pay and not to use any extortion, and does not rather persuade them to leave their calling? Wherefore did

Saint Peter baptize Cornelius the Centurion, who was the first-fruits of the Gentiles? From whence comes it that he did not in any sort whatsoever counsel him to leave his charge?

Now, if to bear arms and to make war be a thing lawful, can there possibly be found any war more just than that which is taken in hand by the command of the superior for the defense of the church, and the preservation of the faithful? Is there any greater tyranny than that which is exercised over the soul? Can there be imagined a war more commendable than that which suppresses such a tyranny? For the last point, I would willingly know of these men whether it be absolutely prohibited Christians to make war upon any occasion whatsoever? If they say that it is forbidden them, from whence comes it then that the men at arms, captains and centurions, who had no other employment but the managing of arms, were always received into the church? Wherefore do the ancient Fathers and Christian historians make so horrible mention of certain legions composed wholly of Christian soldiers, and amongst others of that of Malta, so renowned for the victory which they obtained, and of that of Thebes, of the which Saint Mauritius was general, who suffered martyrdom together with all his troops for the confessing of the name of Jesus Christ? And if it be permitted to make war (as it may be they will confess) to keep the limits and towns of a country and to repulse an invading enemy, is it not yet a thing much more reasonable to take arms to preserve and defend honest men, to suppress the wicked, and to keep and defend the limits and bounds of the church, which is the kingdom of Jesus Christ? If it were otherwise, to what purpose should Saint John have foretold that the whore of Babylon shall be finally ruined by the ten kings, whom she has bewitched? Furthermore, if we hold a contrary opinion, what shall we say of the wars of Constantine against Maxentius and Licimius, celebrated by so many public orations and approved by the testimony of an infinite number of learned men? What opinion should we hold of the many voyages made by Christian princes against the Turks and Saracens to conquer the Holy Land, who had not, or at the least ought not to have had any other end in their designs but to hinder the enemy from ruining the temple of the land, and to restore the integrity of His service into those countries?

Although then the church be not increased by arms, notwithstanding it may be justly preserved by the means of arms. I say further that those that die in so holy a war are no less the martyrs of Jesus Christ than their brethren who were put to death for religion; nay, they who die in that war seem to have this disadvantage: that with a free will and knowing sufficiently hazard, into which they cast themselves, notwithstanding, do courageously expose their lives to death and danger, whereas the others do only not refuse death when it behooves them to suffer. The Turks strive to advance their opinion by the means of arms, and if they do subdue a country, they presently bring in by force the impieties of Muhammad, who in his Koran hath so recommended arms, as they are not ashamed to say it is the ready way to heaven, yet do the Turks constrain no man in matter of conscience. But he who is a much greater adversary to Christ and true religion, with all those kings whom he has enchanted, opposes fire and faggots to the light of the gospel, tortures the Word of God, compelling by wracking and torments as much as in him lies all men to become idolaters, and finally is not ashamed to advance and maintain their faith and law by perfidious disloyalty, and their traditions by continual treasons.

Now on the contrary, those good princes and magistrates are said properly to defend themselves who environ and fortify by all their means and industry the vine of Christ, already planted, to be planted in places where it has not yet been, lest the wild boar of the forest should spoil or devour it. They do this (I say) in covering with their buckler and defending with their sword those who by the preaching of the gospel have been converted to true religion, and in fortifying with their best ability by ravelins, ditches, and rampers the temple of God built with living stones, until it have attained the full height, in despite of all the furious assaults of the enemies thereof. We have lengthened out this discourse thus far to the end we might take away all scruple concerning this question. Set, then, the estates and all the officers of a kingdom, or the greatest part of them, every one established in authority by the people: know, that if they contain not within his bounds (or at the least, employ not the utmost of their endeavors thereto) a king who seeks to corrupt the law of God, or hinders the re- establishment thereof, that they offend grievously against the Lord with whom they have contracted covenants upon those conditions. Those of a town, or of a province, making a portion of a kingdom, let them know also that they draw upon themselves the judgment of God if they drive not impiety out of their walls and confines if the king seek to bring it in, or if they be wanting to preserve by all means, the pure doctrine of the Gospel, although for the defense thereof, they suffer for a time banishment or any other misery. Finally, more private men must be all advertised that nothing can excuse them if they obey any in that which offends God, and that yet they have no right nor warrant, neither may in any sort by their private authority take arms, if it appear not most evidently that they have extraordinary vocation thereunto, all which our discourse will suppose we have confirmed by pregnant testimonies drawn from holy writ.

THE THIRD QUESTION

Whether it be lawful to resist a prince who does oppress or ruin a public state, and how far such resistance may be extended: by whom, how, and by what right or law it is permitted.

Forsomuch as we must here dispute of the lawful authority of a lawful prince, I am confident that this question will be the less acceptable to tyrants and wicked princes; for it is no marvel if those who receive no law but what their own will and fancy dictate unto them, be deaf unto the voice of that law which is grounded upon reason. But I persuade myself that good princes will willingly entertain this discourse, insomuch as they sufficiently know that all magistrates, be they of never so high a rank, are but an inanimated and speaking law. Neither though anything be pressed home against the bad can it fall within any inference against the good kings or princes, as also good and bad princes are in a direct diameter opposite and contrary. Therefore that which shall be urged against tyrants is so far from detracting anything from kings as on the contrary, the more tyrants are laid open in their proper colors, the more glorious does the true worth and dignity of kings appear; neither can the vicious imperfections of the one be laid open, but it gives addition of perfections and respect to the honor of the other.

But for tyrants, let them say and think what they please; that shall be the least of my care, for it is not to them but against them that I write. For kings I believe that they will readily consent to that which is propounded, for by true proportion of reason they ought as much to hate tyrants and wicked governors as shepherds hate wolves; physicians, poisoners; true prophets, false teachers; for it must necessarily occur that reason infuses into good kings as much hatred against tyrants as nature imprints in dogs against wolves, for as the one lives by rapine and spoil, so the other is born or bred to redress and prevent all such outrages. It may be the flatterers of tyrants will cast a supercilious aspect on these lines, but if they were not past all grace they would rather blush for shame. I very well know that the friends and faithful servants of kings will not only approve and lovingly entertain this discourse, but also with their best abilities defend the contents thereof. Accordingly as the reader shall find himself moved either with content or dislike in the reading hereof, let him know that by that he shall plainly discover either the affection or hatred that he bears to tyrants. Let us now enter into the matter.

I. KINGS ARE MADE BY THE PEOPLE

We have showed before that it is God that does appoint kings, who chooses them, who gives the kingdom to them; now we say that the people establish kings, put the scepter into their hands, and who with their suffrages approves the election. God would have it done in this manner, to the end that the kings should acknowledge that after God they hold their power and sovereignty from the people, and that it might the rather induce them to apply and address the utmost of their care and thoughts for the profit of the people, without being puffed with any vain imagination that they were formed of any matter more excellent than other men, for which they were raised so high above others; as if they were to command our flocks of sheep or herds of cattle. But let them remember and know that they are of the same mold and condition as others, raised from the earth by the voice and acclamations, now as it were upon the shoulders of the people unto their thrones, that they might afterwards bear on their own shoulders the greatest burdens of the commonwealth. Divers ages before that the people of Israel demanded a king. God gave and appointed the law of royal government contained in the seventeenth chapter, verse fourteen of Deuteronomy: "When," says Moses, "you are come unto the land which the Lord your God gives you, and shall possess it, and shall dwell therein, and shall say, 'I will set a king over me like as all the nations that are about me,' you shall in any wise set him whom the Lord thy God shall choose from amongst thy brethren, etc." You see here that the election of the king is attributed to God, the establishment to the people: now when the practice of this law came in use, see in what manner they proceeded.

The elders of Israel, who presented the whole body of the people (under this name of elders are comprehended the captains, the centurions, commanders over fifties and tens, judges, provosts, but principally the chiefest of tribes) came to meet Samuel in Ramah, and not being willing longer to endure the government of the sons of Samuel, whose ill carriage had justly drawn on them the people's dislike, and withal persuading themselves that they had found the means to make their wars hereafter with more advantage, they demanded a king of Samuel, who asking counsel of the Lord, he made known that He had chosen Saul for the governor of His people. Then Samuel anointed Saul and performed all those rights which belong to the election of a king required by the people. Now this might, perhaps, have seemed sufficient if Samuel had presented to the people the king who was chosen by God and had admonished them all to become good and obedient subjects. Notwithstanding, to the end that the king might know that he was established by the people, Samuel appointed the estates to meet at Mizpah, where being assembled as if the business were but then to begin, and nothing had already been done, to be brief, as if the election of Saul were then only to be treated of, the lot is cast and falls on the tribe of Benjamin, after on the family of Matri, and lastly on Saul, born of that family, who was the same whom God had chosen. Then by the consent of all the people Saul was declared king. Finally, that Saul nor any other might attribute the aforesaid business to chance or lot, after that Saul had made some proof of his valor in raising the siege of the Ammonites in Jabesh Gilead, some of the people pressing the business, he was again confirmed king in a full assembly at Gilgal. You see that he whom God had chosen and the lot had separated from all the rest is established king by the suffrages of the people.

And for David, by the commandment of God, and in a manner more evident than the former, after the rejection of Saul, Samuel anointed for king over Israel, David, chosen by the Lord, which being done, the Spirit of the Lord presently left Saul and wrought in a special manner in David. But David, notwithstanding, reigns not, but was compelled to save himself in deserts and rocks, oftentimes falling upon the very brim of destruction, and never reigned as king until after the death of Saul; for then by the suffrages of all the people of Judah he was first chosen king of Judah, and seven years after by the consent of all Israel he was inaugurated king of Israel in Hebron. So then he is anointed first by the prophet at the commandment of God, as a token he was chosen, secondly by the commandment of the people when he was established king, and that to the end that kings may always remember that it is from God, but by the people and for the people's sake that they do reign, and that in their glory they say not (as is their custom) they hold their kingdom only of God and their sword, but withal add that it was the people who first girt them with that sword.

The same order offered in Solomon. Although he was the king's son, God had chosen Solomon to sit upon the throne of his kingdom and by express words had promised David to be with him and assist him as a father his son. David had with his own mouth designed Solomon to be successor to his crown in the presence of some of the principal of his court. But this was not enough, and therefore David assembled at Jerusalem the princes of Israel, the heads of the tribes, the captains of the soldiers, and ordinance officers of the kings, the centurions and other magistrates of towns, together with his sons, the noblemen and worthiest person ages of the kingdom to consult and resolve upon the election. In this assembly, after they had called upon the name of God, Solomon, by the consent of the whole congregation, was proclaimed and anointed for king, and sat (so says the text) upon the throne of Israel; then, and not before, the princes, the noblemen, his brothers themselves do him homage and take the oath of allegiance. And to the end that it may not be said that that was only done to avoid occasion of difference which might arise amongst the brothers and sons of David about the succession, we read that the other following kings have, in the same manner been established in their places. It is said that after the death of Solomon, the people assembled to create his son Rehoboam king. After Amaziah was killed, Uzziah, his only son, was chosen king by all the people, Ahaziah after Joram, Joachim, the son of Josiah, after the decease of his father, whose piety might well seem to require that without any other solemnity, notwithstanding, both he and the other were chosen and invested into the royal throne by the suffrages of the people.

To which also belongs, that which Hushai said to Absalom: "Nay, but whom the Lord and His people, and all the men of Israel chose, his will I be, and with him will I abide," which is as much as to say I will follow the king lawfully established, and according to the accustomed order; wherefore, although God had promised to His people a perpetual lamp, to wit, a king, and a continual successor of the line of David, and that the successor of the kings of this people were approved by the Word of God Himself, notwithstanding, we see that the kings have not reigned before the people had ordained and installed them with requisite ceremonies. It may be collected from this that the kingdom of Israel was not hereditary, if we consider David and the promise made to him, and that it was wholly elective, if we regard the particular persons. But to what purpose is this but to make it apparent that the election is only mentioned that the kings might have always in their remembrance that they were raised to their dignities by the people, and therefore they should never forget during life in what a strict bound of observance they are tied to those from whom they have received all their greatness. We read that the kings of the heathen have been established also by the people; for as when they had either troubles at home, or wars abroad, someone, in whose ready valor and discreet integrity the people did principally rely and repose their greatest confidence, him they presently, with an universal consent, constituted king.

Cicero says that amongst the Medes, Diodes, from a judge of private controversies, was for his uprightness by the whole people elected king, and in the same manner were the first kings chosen amongst the Romans. Insomuch that after the death of Romulus, the interreign and government of the hundred senators being little acceptable to the Quirites, it was agreed that from thenceforward the king should be chosen by the suffrages of the people and the approbation of the senate. Tarquinius Superbus was therefore esteemed a tyrant, because being chosen neither by the people nor the senate, he intruded himself into the kingdom only by force and usurpation. Wherefore Julius Caesar, long after, though he gained the empire by the sword, yet to the end he might add some shadow or pretense of right to his former intrusion, he caused himself to be declared, both by the people and senate, perpetual dictator. Augustus, his adopted son, would never take on him as inheritor of the empire although he was declared so by the testaments of Caesar, but always held it as of the people and senate. The same also did Tiberius, Caligula, and Claudius, and the first that assumed the empire to himself without any color of right was Nero, who also by the senate was condemned.

Briefly, forsomuch as none were ever born with crowns on their heads and scepters in their hands, and that no man can be a king by himself, nor reign without people, whereas on the contrary the people may subsist of themselves, and were, long before they had any kings, it must of necessity follow that kings were at the first constituted by the people, and although the sons and dependents of such kings, inheriting their fathers' virtues, may in a sort seem to have rendered their kingdoms hereditary to their offsprings, and that in some kingdoms and countries the right of free election seems in a sort buried, yet, notwithstanding in all well-ordered kingdoms this custom is yet remaining. The sons do not succeed the fathers before the people have first, as it were, anew established them by their new approbation; neither were they acknowledged in quality as inheriting it from the dead, but approved and accounted kings then only, when they were invested with the kingdom by receiving the scepter and diadem from the hands of those who represent the majesty of the people. One may see most evident marks of this in Christian kingdoms which are at this day esteemed hereditary; for the French king, he of Spain and England, and others are commonly sacred and, as it were, put into possession of their authority by the peers, lords of the kingdom, and officers of the crown, who represent the body of the people, no more nor less than the emperors of Germany are chosen by the electors, and the kings of Polonia, by the yawodes and palatines of the kingdom, where the right of election is yet in force.

In like manner also, the cities give no royal reception, nor entries unto the king, but after their inauguration, and anciently they used not to count the times of their reign but from the day of their coronation, the which was strictly observed in France. But lest the continued course of some successions should deceive us, we must take notice that the estates of the kingdoms have often preferred the cousin before the son, the younger brother before the elder, as in France Louis was preferred before his brother Robert, Earl of Eureux [Annales Gillii]; in like manner Henry before Robert, nephew to Capet. Nay, which is more by authority of the people in the same kingdom, the crown has been transported (the lawful inheritors living) from one lineage to another, as from that of Merove to that of the Charlemagnes, and from that of the Charlemagnes, to that of the Capets, the which has also been done in other kingdoms, as the best historians testify.

But not to wander from France, the long continuance and power of which kingdom may in some sort plead for a ruling authority and where succession seems to have obtained most reputation. We read that Pharamond was chosen in the year 419, Pepin in the year 751, Charles the Great and Charlemagne, the son of Pepin in the year 768, without having any respect to their fathers' former estate. Charlemagne dying in the year 772, his portion fell not presently into the possession of his brother Charles the Great as it ordinarily happens in the succession of inheritances, but by the ordinance of the people and the estates of the kingdom he is invested with it; the same author witnesses that in the year 812, Lewis the Courteous, although he was the son of Charles the Great, was also elected, and in the testament of Charlemagne, inserted into the history written by Nauclerus, Charlemagne does entreat the people to choose, by a general assembly of the estates of the kingdom, which of his grandchildren or nephews the people pleased, and commanding the uncles to observe and obey the ordinance of the people, by means whereof, Charles the Bold, nephew to Louis the Courteous and Judith, declares himself to be chosen king, as Aimonius the French historian recites.

To conclude, in a word, all kings at the first were altogether elected, and those who at this day seem to have their crowns and royal authority by inheritance, have or should have, first and principally their confirmation from the people. Briefly, although the people of some countries have been accustomed to choose their kings of such a lineage, which for some notable merits have worthily deserved it, yet we must believe that they choose the stock itself, and not every branch that proceeds from it; neither are they so tied to that election, as if the successor degenerate, they may not choose another more worthy; neither those who come and are the next of that stock, are born kings, but created such, nor called kings, but princes of the blood royal.

II. THE WHOLE BODY OF THE PEOPLE IS ABOVE THE KING

N ow, seeing that the people choose and establish their kings, it follows that the whole body of the people is above the king; for it is a thing most evident that he who is established by another is accounted under him who has established him, and he who receives his authority from another is less than he from whom he derives his power. Potiphar the Egyptian sets Joseph over all his house; Nebuchadnezzar, Daniel over the province of Babylon; Darius the six score governors over the kingdom. It is commonly said that masters establish their servants, kings their officers. In like manner, also, the people establish the king as administrator of the commonwealth. Good kings have not disdained this title; yea, the bad ones themselves have affected it, insomuch as for the space of divers ages, no Roman emperor (if it were not some absolute tyrant, as Nero, Domitian, Caligula) would suffer himself to be called lord. Furthermore, it must necessarily be that kings were instituted for the people's sake; neither can it be that for the pleasure of some hundreds of men, and without doubt more foolish and worse than many of the others, all the rest were made, but much rather that these hundred were made for the use and service of all the others, and reason requires that he be preferred above the others, who was made only to and for his occasion; so it is that for the ship's sail, the owner appoints a pilot over her, who sits at the helm and looks that she keep her course, nor run not upon any dangerous shelf; the pilot doing his duty, is obeyed by the mariners, yea, and of himself who is owner of the vessel, notwithstanding the pilot is a servant as well as the least in the ship, from whom he only differs in this: that he serves in a better place than they do.

In a commonwealth, commonly compared to a ship, the king holds the place of pilot, the people in general are owners of the vessel, obeying the pilot, whilst he is careful of the public good, as though this pilot neither is nor ought to be esteemed other than servant to the public, as a judge or general in war differs little from other officers, but that he is bound to bear greater burdens and expose himself to more dangers. By the same reason also which the king gains by acquisition of arms, be it that he possesses himself of frontier places in warring on the enemy, or that which he gets by escheats or confiscations, he gets it to the kingdom, and not to himself, to wit, to the people of whom the kingdom is composed, no more nor less than the servant does for his master; neither may one contract or oblige themselves to him, but by and with reference to the authority derived from the people. Furthermore, there is an infinite sort of people who live without a king, but we cannot imagine a king without people. And those who have been raised to the royal dignity were not advanced because they excelled other men in beauty and comeliness, nor in some excellency of nature to govern them as shepherds do their flocks, but rather being made out of the same mass with the rest of the people, they should acknowledge that for them, they, as it were, borrow their power and authority.

The ancient custom of the French represents that exceedingly well, for they used to lift up on a buckler, and salute him king whom they had chosen. And wherefore is it said, "I pray you, that kings have an infinite number of eyes, a million of ears, with extreme long hands, and feet exceeding swift?" Is it because they are like to Argos, Gerien, Midas, and divers others so celebrated by the poets? No, truly, but it is said in regard of all the people, whom the business principally concerns, who lend to the king for the good of the commonwealth their eyes, their ears, their means, their faculties. Let the people forsake the king, he presently falls to the ground, although before, his hearing and sight seemed most excellent, and that he was strong and in the best disposition that might be; yea, that he seemed to triumph in all magnificence, yet in an instant he will become most vile and contemptible. To be brief, instead of those divine honors wherewith all men adore him, he shall be compelled to become a pedant, and whip children in the school at Corinth. Take away but the basis to this giant, and like the Rhodian Colossus, he presently tumbles on the ground and falls into pieces. Seeing then that the king is established in this degree by the people, and for their sake, and that he cannot subsist without them, who can think it strange, then, for us to conclude that the people are above the king?

Now that which we speak of all the people universally ought also to be understood as has been delivered in the second question of those who in every kingdom or town do lawfully represent the body of the people and who ordinarily (or at least should be) called the officers of the kingdom or of the crown, and not of the king; for the officers of the king, it is he who places and displaces them at his pleasure, yea, after his death they have no more power and are accounted as dead. On the contrary, the officers of the kingdom receive their authority from the people in the general assembly of the states (or, at the least were accustomed so anciently to have done) and cannot be disauthorized but by them, so then the one depends of the king, the other of the kingdom, those of the sovereign officer of the kingdom, who is the king himself, those of the sovereignty itself, that is of the people, of which sovereignty, both the king and all his officers of the kingdom ought to depend, the charge of the one has proper relation to the care of the king's person; that of the other, to look that the commonwealth receive no damage; the first ought to serve and assist the king, as all domestic servants are bound to do to their masters; the other to preserve the rights and privileges of the people, and to carefully hinder the prince that he neither omit the things that may advantage the state, nor commit anything that may endamage the public.

Briefly, the one are servants and domestics of the king, and received into their places to obey his person; the other, on the contrary, are as associates to the king in the administration of justice, participating of the royal power and authority, being bound to the utmost of their power to be assisting in the managing of the affairs of state, as well as the king, who is, as it were, president amongst them, and principal only in order and degree.

Therefore, as all the whole people is above the king, and likewise taken in one entire body, are in authority before him, yet being considered one by one, they are all of them under the king. It is easy to know how far the power of the first kings extended, in that Ephron, king of the Hittites, could not grant Abraham the sepulcher, but in the presence, and with the consent of the people; neither could Hamor the Hivite, king of Shechem, contract an alliance with Jacob without the people's assent and confirmation thereof, because it was then the custom to refer the most important affairs to be dispensed and resolved in the general assemblies of the people. This might easily be practiced in those kingdoms which were then almost confined within the circuit of one town.

But since the kings began to extend their limits, and that it was impossible for the people to assemble together all into one place because of their great numbers, which would have occasioned confusion, the officers of the kingdom were established, who should ordinarily preserve the rights of the people in such sort notwithstanding, as when extraordinary occasion required, the people might be assembled, or at the least such an abridgment as might by the most principal members be a representation of the whole body. We see this order established in the kingdom of Israel, which (in the judgment of the wisest politicians) was excellently ordered. The king had his cup-bearers, his carvers, his chamberlains and stewards. The kingdom had her officers, to wit, the seventy-one elders, and the heads and chief chosen out of all the tribes, who had the care of the public faith in peace and war.

Furthermore, the kingdom had in every town magistrates, who had the particular government of them, as the former were for the whole kingdom. At such times as affairs of consequence were to be treated of, they assembled together, but nothing that concerned the public state could receive any solid determination. David assembled the officers of his kingdom when he desired to invest his son Solomon with the royal dignity; when he would have examined and approved that manner of policy, and managing of affairs that he had revived and restored; and when there was no question of removing the ark of the covenant. And because they represented the whole people, it is said in the history that all the people assembled. These were the same officers who delivered Jonathan from death, condemned by the sentence of the king, by which it appears that there might be an appeal from the king to the people.

After that the kingdom was divided through the pride of Rehoboam. The council at Jerusalem composed of seventy-one ancients seems to have such authority that they might judge the king as well as the king might judge every one of them in particular. In this council was president the duke of the house of Judah, to wit, some principal man chosen out of that tribe; as also, in the city of Jerusalem, there was a governor chosen out of the tribe of Benjamin residing there. This will appear more manifest by examples: Jeremiah was sent by God to denounce to the Jews the destruction of Jerusalem, and was therefore condemned first by the priests and prophets, in whose hands was the ecclesiastical jurisdiction, afterwards by all the people of the city, that is, by the ordinary judges of Jerusalem, to wit, the

milleniers and the centurions. Finally, the matter being brought before the princes of Judah, who were the seventy-one elders assembled,
and set near to the new gate of the temple, he was by them acquitted.
In this very assembly, they did discreetly condemn in express terms
the wicked and cruel act of the king Jehoiakim, who a little before had
caused the prophet Uriah to be slain, who also foretold the destruction of Jerusalem.

We read in another place that Zedekiah held in such reverence the
authority of this council that he was so far from delivering of Jeremiah from the dungeon, whereunto the seventy-one had cast him,
that he dared scarce remove him into a less rigorous prison. They persuading him to give his consent to the putting to death the prophet
Jeremiah, he answered that he was in their hands and that he might
not oppose them in anything. The same king, fearing lest they might
make information against him to bring him to an account for certain
speeches he had used with the prophet Jeremiah, was glad to feign an
untrue excuse. It appears by this that in the kingdom of Judah this
council was above the king, in this kingdom, I say, not fashioned or
established by Plato or Aristotle, but by the Lord God Himself, being
author of all their order, and supreme moderator in that monarchy.
Such were the seven magi or sages in the Persian empire, who had
almost a paralleled dignity with the king and were termed the ears
and eyes of the king, who also never dissented from the judgment of
those sages.

In the kingdom of Sparta there were the ephori, to whom an appeal lay from the judgment of the king, and who, as Aristotle says,
had authority also to judge the kings themselves. In Egypt the people
were accustomed to choose and give officers to the king, to the end
they might hinder and prevent any encroachment or usurped authority contrary to the laws. Now as Aristotle does ordinarily term those
lawful kings who have for their assistants such officers or counselors,
so also makes he no difficulty to say that where they be wanting, there

can be no true monarchy, but rather a tyranny absolutely barbarous, or at the least such a dominion as does most nearly approach tyranny.

In the Roman commonwealth, such were the senators and the magistrates created by the people, the tribune of those who were called Celeres, the praetor or provost of the city, and others, insomuch as there lay an appeal from the king to the people, as Seneca declares by divers testimonies drawn from Cicero's books of the commonwealth, and the history of Oratius sufficiently shows, who being condemned by the judges for killing his sister was acquitted by the people. In the times of the emperors, there was the senate, the consuls, the praetors, the great provosts of the empire, the governors of provinces, attributed to the senate and the people, all which were called the magistrates and officers of the people of Rome. And therefore when by the decree of the senate, the emperor Maximus was declared enemy of the commonwealth, and Maximus and Albinus were created emperors by the senate, the men of war were sworn to be faithful and obedient to the people of Rome, the senate, and the emperors. Now for the empires and public states of these times (except those of Turkey, Muscovy and such like, which are rather a rhapsody of robbers and barbarous intruders than any lawful empires), there is not one which is not or hath not heretofore been governed in the manner we have described. And if through the convenience and sloth of the principal officers the successors have found the business in a worse condition, those who have for the present the public authority in their hands are notwithstanding bound as much as in them lies to reduce things into their primary estate and condition.

In the empire of Germany, which is conferred by election, there are the electors and the princes, both secular and ecclesiastical, the counts, barons, and deputies of the imperial cities, and as all these in their proper places are solicitors for the public good, likewise in the diets do they represent the majesty of the empire, being obliged to advise and carefully foresee that neither by the emperor's partiality,

hate, nor affection the public state do suffer or be interested. And for
this reason, the empire has its chancellor, as well as the emperor his,
and both the one and the other have their peculiar officers and treasurers apart. And it is a thing so notorious that the empire is preferred
before the emperor that it is a common saying, "That emperor does
homage to the empire."

In like manner, in the kingdom of Polonia, there are for officers
of the crown the bishops, the palatines, the castellains, the nobility,
the deputies of towns and provinces assembled extraordinarily, before whom and with whose consent, and nowhere else, they make
new laws and determinations concerning wars. For the ordinary government there are the counselors of the kingdom, the chancellor of
the state, etc., although notwithstanding, the king has his stewards,
chamberlains, servants, and domestics. Now if any man should demand in Polonia who were the greater, the king or all the people of
the kingdom, represented by the lords and magistrates, he should do
as much, as if he asked at Venice if the duke were above the seigniory.
But what shall we say of kingdoms which are said to go by hereditary
succession? We may indeed conclude the very same. The kingdom of
France heretofore preferred before all others, both in regard of the excellency of their laws and majesty of their estate, may pass with most
as a ruling case. Now, although those who have the public commands
in their hands do not discharge their duties as were to be desired, it
follows not though that they are not bound to do it. The king has his
high steward of his household, his chamberlains, his masters of his
games, cup-bearers, and others, whose offices were wont so to depend
on the person of the king that after that the death of their master,
their offices were void. And indeed at the funeral of the king, the lord
high steward in the presence of all the officers and servants of the
household breaks his staff of office and says, "Our master is dead: let
everyone provide for himself." On the other side, the kingdom has
her officers, to wit, the mayor of the palace, who since has been called

the constable, the marshals, the admiral, the chancellor, or great referendary, the secretaries, the treasurers and others, who heretofore were created in the assembly of the three estates: the clergy, the nobility, and the people.

Since the parliament of Paris was made sedentary, they are not thought to be established in their places before they have been first received and approved by that course of parliament, and may not be dismissed nor disposed but by the authority and consent of the same. Now all these officers take their oath to the kingdom, which is as much as to say to the people in the first place, then to the king who is protector of the kingdom, the which appears by the tenure of the oath. Above all, the constable who, receiving the sword from the king, has it girded unto him with this charge, that he maintain and defend the commonwealth, as appears by the words that the king then pronounces.

Besides, the kingdom of France has the peers (so called either for that they are the king's companions, or because they are the fathers of the commonwealth) taking their denominations from the several provinces of the kingdom, in whose hands the king at his inauguration takes his oath as if all the people of the kingdom were in them present, which shows that these twelve peers are above the king. They on the other side swear that they will preserve not the king, but the crown; that they will assist the commonwealth with their counsel, and therefore will be present with their best abilities to counsel the prince both in peace and war, as appears plainly in the patentee of their peership. And they therefore have the same right as the peers of the court, who according to the law of the Lombards were not only associates to the lord of the fee in the judgment of causes, but also did take an account and judge the differences that happened between the lord and his vassals.

We may also know that those peers of France did often discuss suits and differences between the king and his subjects, insomuch that when Charles the Sixth would have given sentence against the Duke of Brittany, they opposed it, alleging that the discussing of that business belonged properly to the peers and not to the king, who might not in any sort derogate from their authority. Therefore it is that yet at this day the parliament of Paris is called the court of peers, being in some sort constituted judge between the king and the people, yea, between the king and every private person, and is bound and ought to maintain the meanest in the kingdom against the king's attorney, if he undertake anything contrary to law.

Furthermore, if the king ordain anything in his council, if he treat any agreement with the princes his neighbors, if he begin a war or make peace, as lately with Charles the Fifth the emperor the parliament ought to interpose their authority, and all that which concerns the public state must be therein registered; neither is there anything firm and stable which the parliament does not first approve. And to the end that the counselors of that parliament should not fear the king, formerly they attained not to that place, but by the nomination of the whole body of the court; neither could they be dismissed for any lawful cause, but by the authority of the said body.

Furthermore, if the letters of the king be not sub-signed by a secretary of the kingdom, at this day called a secretary of state, and if the letters patent be not sealed by the chancellor who has power also to cancel them, they are of no force or value. There are also dukes, marquesses, earls, viscounts, barons, seneschals, and, in the cities and good towns, mayors, bailiffs, lieutenants, capitols, consuls, syndics, sheriffs and others, who have special authority, through the circuit of some countries or towns to preserve the people of their jurisdiction. Time it is that at this day some of these dignities are become hereditary. Thus much concerning the ordinary magistrates.

III. THE ASSEMBLY OF THE THREE ESTATES

B esides all this, anciently every year and since less often, to wit, when some urgent necessity required it, the general or three estates were assembled, where all the provinces and towns of any worth, to wit, the burgesses, nobles and ecclesiastical persons, did all of them send their deputies, and there they did publicly deliberate and conclude of that which concerned the public state. Always the authority of this assembly was such that what was there determined, whether it were to treat peace, or make war, or create a regent in the kingdom, or impose some new tribute, it was ever held firm and inviolable, nay, which is more by the authority of this assembly, the kings convinced of loose intemperance or of insufficiency, for so great a charge or tyranny were disthronized, yea, their whole races were forever excluded from their succession to the kingdom, no more nor less as their progenitors were by the same authority formerly called to that administration of the same kingdom. Those whom the consent and approbation of the estates had formerly raised were by the dissent and disallowing of the same afterwards cast down. Those who, tracing in the virtuous steps of their ancestors, were called to that dignity, as if it had been their inheritance, were driven out and disinherited for their degenerate ingratitude, and for that being tainted with insupportable vices, they made themselves incapable and unworthy of such honor.

This shews that succession was tolerated to avoid practices, close and underhand canvassing, discontents of persons refused, contentions, interreigns, and other discommodities of elections. But on the other part, when successions brought other mischiefs more pernicious, when tyranny trampled on the kingdom, and when a tyrant possessed himself of the royal throne, the medicine proving much worse than the disease, then the estates of the kingdom lawfully assembled in the name of all the people have ever maintained their authority, whether it were to drive out a tyrant, or other unworthy king, or to establish a good one in his place. The ancient French had learned that of the Gauls, as Caesar shows in his commentaries. For Ambiorix, king of the Eburons, or Leigeons confesses that such was the condition of the Gaulish empire that people lawfully assembled had no less power over the king than the king had over the people. The which appears also in Vercingetorix, who gives an account of his actions before the assembly of the people.

In the kingdoms of Spain, especially Arragon, Valentia, and Catalonia, there is the very same. For that which is called the Justitia Major in Arragon has the sovereign authority in itself. And there, the lords who represent the people proceed so far that both at the inauguration of the king, as also at the assembly of the estates, which is observed every third year, they say to the king in express words that which follows, "We who are as much worth as you and have more power than you choose you king upon these and these conditions, and there is one between you and us who commands over you, to wit, the Justitia Major of Arragon, who oftentimes refuses that which the king demands, and forbids that which the king enjoins."

In the kingdoms of England and Scotland the sovereignty seems to be in the parliament, which heretofore was held almost every year. They call parliaments the assembly of the estates of the kingdom, in the which the bishops, earls, barons, deputies of towns and provinces deliver their opinions, and resolve with a joint consent of the affairs of state. The authority of this assembly has been so sacred and inviolable that the king dare not abrogate or alter that which had been there once decreed. It was that which heretofore called and installed in their charges all the chief officers of the kingdom, yea, and sometimes the ordinary councilors of that which they call the king's privy council. In some, the other Christian kingdoms, as Hungary, Bohemia, Denmark, Sweden, and the rest, they have their officers apart from the kings, and histories, together with the examples that we have in these our times, sufficiently demonstrate that these officers and estates have known how to make use of their authority, even to the deposing and driving out of the tyrannous and unworthy kings.

We must not therefore esteem that this cuts too short the wings of royal authority, and that it is as much as to take the king's head from his shoulders.

We believe that God is almighty, neither think we it anything diminishes His power because He cannot sin; neither say we that His empire is less to be esteemed, because it cannot be neither shaken, nor cast down; neither also must we judge a king to be too much abused if he be withheld by others from falling into an error, to which he is over much inclined, or for that by the wisdom and discretion of some of his counselors his kingdom is preserved and kept entire and safe, which otherwise, haply by his weakness or wickedness, might have been ruined. Will you say that a man is less healthy because he is environed with discreet physicians, who counsel him to avoid all intemperance, and forbid him to eat such meats as are obnoxious to the stomach, and who purge him many times against his will, and when he resists, who will prove his better friends, these physicians who are studiously careful of his health, or those sycophants who are ready at every turn to give him that which must of necessity hasten his end? We must then always observe this distinction. The first are the friends of the king. The other are the friends of Francis who is king. The friends of Francis are those who serve him. The friends of the king are the officers and servants of the kingdom. For, seeing the king has this name, because of the kingdom, and that it is the people who give being and consistence to the kingdom, the which being lost or ruined, he must needs cease to be a king, or at the least not so truly a king, or else we must take a shadow for a substance.

Without question, those are most truly the king's friends who are most industriously careful of the welfare of his kingdom, and those his worst enemies who neglect the good of the commonwealth, and seek to draw the king into the same lapse of error.

And, as it is impossible to separate the kingdom from the people, nor the king from the kingdom, in like manner, neither can the friends of the king be disjoined from the friends of the people, and the kingdom. I say, further, that those who with a true affection love Francis had rather see him a king than a subject. Now, seeing they cannot see him a king, it necessarily follows that in loving Francis they must also love the kingdom. But those who would be esteemed more the friends of Francis than of the kingdom and the people are truly flatterers, and the most pernicious enemies of the king and public state. Now, if they were true friends indeed, they would desire and endeavor that the king might become more powerful, and more assured in his estate according to that notable saying of Theopompus, king of Sparta, after the ephores or controllers of the kings were instituted. "The more," said he "are appointed by the people to watch over, and look to the affairs of the kingdom, the more those who govern shall have credit, and the more safe and happy shall be the state."

IV. WHETHER TIME'S PRESCRIPTION REMOVES THE PEOPLE'S RIGHT

B ut peradventure, someone will reply, you speak to us here of peers, of lords and officers of the crown. But I, for my part, see not any, but only some shows and shadows of antiquity as if they were to be represented on a stage. I see not for the present scarce any tract of that ancient liberty and authority, nay, which is worse, a great part, if not all of those officers take care of nothing but their particular affairs and almost, if not altogether, serve as flatterers about those kings who jointly toss the poor people like tennis balls; hardly is there one to be found who has compassion on or will lend a helping hand to the miserable subjects, fleeced and scorched to the very bones by their insolent and insupportable oppression. If any be but thought to have such a desire, they are presently condemned as rebels and seditious, and are constrained either to fly with much discommodity, or else must run hazard both of life and liberty. What can be answered to this? The business goes thus. The outrageousness of kings, the ignorance of the party, together with the wicked connivance of the great ones of the kingdom, has been for the most part such throughout the world that the licentious and unbridled power wherewith most kings are transported and which has made them insupportable has in a manner by the length of continuance gained right of prescription, and the people, for want of using it, have intacitly quit, if not altogether lost, their just and ancient authority, so that it ordinarily happens that what all men's care ought to attend on is for the most part neglected by every man; for what is committed to the generality, no man thinks is commended to his custody. Notwithstanding, no such prescription nor prevarication can justly prejudice the right of the people. It is commonly said that the exchequers do admit no rule of prescription against it, much less against the whole body of the people, whose power transcends the king's and in whose right the king assumes to himself that privilege; for otherwise, the prince is only administrator, and the people true proprietor of the public exchequer, as we will prove here presently after.

Furthermore, it is not a thing resolved on by all that no tyrannous intrusion or usurpation and continuance in the same course can by any length of time prescribe against lawful liberty. If it be objected that kings were enthronized, and received their authority from the people who lived five hundred years ago, and not by those now living, I answer that the commonwealth never dies, although kings be taken out of this life one after another: for as the continual running of the water gives the river a perpetual being, so the alternative revolution of birth and death renders the people (*quoad hunc mundum*) immortal.

And further, as we have at this day the same Seine and Tiber as was 1,000 years ago, in like manner also is there the same people of Germany, France, and Italy (excepting intermixing of colonies, or such like); neither can the lapse of time, nor changing of individuals alter in any sort the right of those people. Furthermore, they say the king receives his kingdom from his father, and not from the people, and he from his grandfather, and so one from another upward.

I ask, could the grandfather or ancestor transfer a greater right to his successor than he had himself? If he could not (as without doubt it must need be so) is it not plainly perspicuous that what the successor further arrogates to himself, he may usurp with as safe a conscience as what a thief gets by the highwayside? The people, on the contrary, have their right of eviction entire and whole. Although the officers of the crown have for a time lost or left their ranks, this cannot in any true right prejudice the people, but rather clear otherwise, as one would not grant audience or show favor to a slave who had long since held his master prisoner, and did not only vaunt himself to be free, but also presumptuously assumed power over the life and death of his master; neither would any man allow the excuses of a thief, because he had continued in that trade thirty years, or because he had been bred in that course of life by his father, if he presumed by his long continuance in that function to prescribe for the lawfulness; but rather the longer he had continued in his wickedness, the more grievous should be his punishment. In like manner, the prince is altogether unsupportable who, because he succeeds a tyrant or has kept the people (by whose suffrages he holds the crown) in a long slavery, or has suppressed the officers of the kingdom (who should be protectors of the public liberty) that therefore presumes that what he affects is lawful for him to effect and that his will is not to be restrained or corrected by any positive law whatsoever. For prescription in tyranny detracts nothing from the right of the people, nay, it rather much aggravates the prince's outrages. But what if the peers and principal officers of the kingdom make themselves parts with the king? What if betraying the public cause the yoke of tyranny upon the people's neck? Shall it follow that by this prevarication and treason the authority is devolved into the king? Does this detract anything from the right of the people's liberty, or does it add any licentious power to the king? Let the people thank themselves, say you, who relied on the disloyal loyalty of such men.

But I answer, that these officers are indeed those protectors whose principal care and study should be that the people be maintained in the free and absolute fruition of their goods and liberty. And therefore, in the same manner as if a treacherous advocate for a sum of money should agree to betray the cause of his client into the hands of his adversary, which he ought to have defended, has not power for all that to alter the course of justice, nor of a bad cause to make a good one, although perhaps for a time he give some color of it. In like manner this conspiracy of the great ones combined to ruin the inferiors cannot disannul the right of the people. In the mean season, those great ones incur the punishment that the same allots against prevaricators, and for the people, the same law allows them to choose another advocate and afresh to pursue their cause, as if it were then only to begin.

For if the people of Rome condemned their captains and generals of their armies because they capitulated with their enemies to their disadvantage (although they were drawn to it by necessity, being on the point to be all overthrown) and would not be bound to perform the soldiers' capitulation, much less shall a free people be tied up to bear the yoke of thralldom which is cast on them by those who should and might have prevented it; but being neither forced nor compelled did, for their own particular gain, willingly betray those who had committed their liberty to their custody.

V. WHY KINGS WERE CREATED

N ow, seeing that kings have been ever established by the people, and that they have had associates joined with them, to contain them within the limits of their duties, the which associates considered in particular one by one are under the king and altogether in one entire body are above him, we must consequently see wherefore first kings were established, and what is principally their duty. We usually esteem a thing just and good when it attains to the proper end for which it is ordained.

In the first place everyone consents that men by nature loving liberty and hating servitude, born rather to command than obey, have not willingly admitted to be governed by another, and renounced as it were the privilege of nature by submitting themselves to the commands of others, but for some special and great profit that they expected from it. For as Aesop says, that the horse being before accustomed to wander at his pleasure, would never have received the bit into his mouth, nor the rider on his back, but that he hoped by that means to overmatch the bull. Neither let us imagine that kings were chosen to apply to their own proper use the goods that are gotten by the sweat of their subjects; for every man loves and cherishes his own. They have not received the power and authority of the people to make it serve as a pander to their pleasures; for ordinarily, the inferiors hate or at least envy their superiors.

Let us then conclude that they are established in this place to maintain by justice and to defend by force of arms both the public state and particular persons from all damages and outrages; wherefore Saint Augustine said, "Those are properly called lords and masters who provide for the good and profit of others, as the husband for the wife, fathers for their children." They must therefore obey them who provide for them, although, indeed, to speak truly, those who govern in this manner may in a sort be said to serve those whom they command over. For, as says the same doctor, they command not for the desire of dominion, but for the duty they owe to provide for the good of those who are subjected to them, not affecting any lord-like domineering, but with charity and singular affection desiring the welfare of those who are committed to them.

Seneca in the eighty-first epistle says that in the golden age wise men only governed kingdoms: they kept themselves within the bounds of moderation and preserved the meanest from the oppression of the greatest. They persuaded and dissuaded, according as it advantaged or disadvantaged, the public profit; by their wisdom, they furnished the public with plenty of all necessaries, and by their discretion prevented scarcity; by their valor and courage they expelled dangers; by their many benefits they increased and enriched their subjects; they pleaded not their duty in making pompous shows, but in well governing their people. No man-made trial what he was able to do against them, because everyone received what he was capable of from them, etc.

Therefore, then, to govern is nothing else but to provide for. These proper ends of commanding, being for the people's commodity, the only duty of kings and emperors is to provide for the people's good. The kingly dignity to speak properly is not a title of honor, but a weighty and burdensome office. It is not a discharge or vacation from affairs to run a licentious course of liberty, but a charge and vocation to all industrious employments, for the service of the commonwealth, the which has some glimpse of honor with it, because in those first and golden ages no man would have tasted of such continual troubles if they had not been sweetened with some relish of honor; insomuch as there was nothing more true than that which was commonly said in those times: "If every man knew with what turmoils and troubles the royal wreath was wrapped withal, no man would vouchsafe to take it up, although it lay at his feet."

When, therefore, that these words of mine and yours entered into the world, and that differences fell amongst fellow citizens, touching the propriety of goods, and wars amongst neighboring people about the right of their confines, the people bethought themselves to have recourse to someone who both could and should take order that the poor were not oppressed by the rich, nor the patriots wronged by strangers. Nor as wars and suits increased, they chose someone in whose wisdom and valor they reposed most confidence. See, then, wherefore kings were created in the first ages: to wit, to administer justice at home and to be leaders in the wars abroad, and not only to repulse the incursions of the enemy, but also to repress and hinder the devastation and spoiling of the subjects and their goods at home, but above all, to expel and drive away all devices and debauchments far from their dominions. This may be proved by all histories, both divine and profane. For the people of God, they had at first no other king but God Himself, who dwelt in the midst of them and gave answer from between the cherubim, appointed extraordinary judges and captains for the wars, by means whereof the people thought they had no need of lieutenants, being honored by the continual presence of their Sovereign King.

Now, when the people of God began to be aweary of the injustice of the sons of Samuel, on whose old age they dared no longer rely, they demanded a king after the manner of other people, saying to

Samuel, "Give us a king as other people have, that he may judge us" (1 Sam. 8:6). There is touched the first and principal point of the duty of a king, a little after they are both mentioned. "We will have," said they "a king over us like other nations. Our king shall judge us, and go in and out before us, and lead our armies" (1 Sam. 8:20). To do justice is always set in the first place, forsomuch as it is an ordinary and perpetual thing, but wars are extraordinary, and happen as it were casually. Wherefore, Aristotle says that in the time of Herold, all kings were judges and captains. For the Lacedemonian kings, they in his time also had sovereign authority only in the army, and that confined also to the commandments of the ephores. In like manner the Medes, who were ever in perpetual quarrels amongst themselves, at the length chose Deolces for the judge, who had carried himself well in the deciding of some particular differences; presently afterwards they made him king and gave him officers and guards that he might more easily suppress the powerful and insolent.

Cicero says that anciently all kings were established to administer justice, and that their institution and that of the laws had one and the same end, which was that equity and right might be duly rendered to all men, the which may be verified by the propriety of the words almost in all languages. Kings are called by the Latins, *Reges a regendo*, because they must rule and govern the limits and bounds, both of the public and particulars. The names of emperors, princes, and dukes have relation to their conduct in the wars, and principal places in combats and other places of command. Likewise the Greeks call them in their language, Basiles, Archa, Hegomodes, which is to say props of the people, princes, conductors. The Germans and other nations use all significant names, and which express that the duty of a king consists not in making glorious paradoes, but that it is an office of a weighty charge and continual care. But, in brief, the poet Homer calls kings the judges of cities, and in describing Agamemnon, he calls him wise, strong, and valiant. As also, Ovid, speaking of Erechtheus, says that it was hard to know whether justice or valor were more transparent in him, in which these two poets seem exactly to have described the duties of kings and princes. You see what the custom of the kings of the heathen nations was, after whose examples the Jews demanded and established their kings.

The Queen of Sheba said also to Solomon that God had made him king over them to do judgment and justice. And Solomon himself, speaking to God, said, "you hast chosen me to be a king over Thy people, and a judge of Thy sons and daughters" (Wisdom 9:7). For this cause also the good kings, as David, Jehoshaphat, and others, being not able in their own persons to determine all the suits and differences of their subjects (although in the causes of greatest importance they reserved an appeal always to themselves, as appears in Samuel) had ever above all things a special care to establish in all places just and discreet judges, and principally still to have an eye to the right administration of justice, knowing themselves to carry the sword, as well to chastise wicked and unjust subjects as to repulse foreign enemies.

Briefly, as the apostle says, "The prince is ordained by God for the good and profit of the people, being armed with the sword to defend the good from the violence of the wicked, and when he discharges his duty therein, all men owe him honor and obedience."

Seeing then that kings are ordained by God and established by the people to procure and provide for the good of those who are committed unto them, and that this good or profit be principally expressed in two things, to wit, in the administration of justice to their subjects and in the managing of armies for the repulsing their enemies; certainly, we must infer and conclude from this that the prince who applied himself to nothing but his peculiar profits and pleasures or to those ends which most readily conduce thereunto, who condemns and perverts all laws, who uses his subjects more cruelly than the barbarous enemy would do, he may truly and really be called a tyrant, and that those who in this manner govern their kingdoms, be they of never so large an extent are more properly unjust pillagers and free-booters than lawful governors.

VI. WHETHER KINGS BE
ABOVE THE LAW

We must here yet proceed a little further: for it is demand-ed whether the king who presides in the administration of justice has power to resolve and determine business according to his own will and pleasure? Must the kings be subject to the law, or does the law depend upon the king? The law (says an ancient) is respected by those who otherwise contemn virtue, for it enforces obedience and ministers' conduct in warfaring, and gives vigor and luster to justice and equity. Pausanias the Spartan will answer in a word that it be-comes laws to direct and men to yield obedience to their authority. Agesilaus, king of Sparta, says that all commanders must obey the commandments of the laws. But it shall not be amiss to carry this matter a little higher. When people began to seek for justice to deter-mine their differences, if they met with any private man that did just-ly appoint them, they were satisfied with it. Now forsomuch as such men were rarely and with much difficulty met withal, and for that the judgments of kings received as laws were oftentimes found contrary and difficult, then the magistrates and others of great wisdom invent-ed laws, which might speak to all men in one and the same voice.

This being done, it was expressly enjoined to kings that they should be the guardians and administrators, and sometimes also, forsomuch

as the laws could not foresee the particularities of actions to resolve
exactly, it was permitted the king to supply this defect by the same
natural equity by which the laws were drawn, and for fear lest they
should go against law, the people appointed them from time to time
associates, counselors, of whom we have formerly made mention;
wherefore there is nothing which exempts the king from obedience
which he owes to the law, which he ought to acknowledge as his lady
and mistress, esteeming nothing can become him worse than that
feminine of which Juvenal speaks: *Sic volo, sic jubeo, sic pro ratione vol-
untas.* I will, I command, my will shall serve instead of reason. Neither
should they think their authority the less because they are confined
to laws, for seeing the law is a divine gift coming from above, which
human societies are happily governed and addressed to their best and
blessedest end, those kings are as ridiculous and worthy of contempt
who repute it a dishonor to conform themselves to law, as those sur-
veyors who think themselves disgraced, by using of a rule, a compass,
a chain or other instruments, which men understanding the art of
surveying are accustomed to do, or a pilot who had rather fail, according to his fantasy and imagination, than steer his course by his needle
and sea-card. Who can doubt but that it is a thing more profitable
and convenient to obey the law than the king who is but one man?
The law is the soul of a good king: it gives him motion, sense, and
life. The king is the organ and as it were the body by which the law
displays her forces, exercises her function, and expresses her concep-
tions. Now it is a thing much more reasonable to obey the soul than
the body; the law is the wisdom of diverse sages, recollected in few
words, but many see more clear and further than one alone. It is much
better to follow the law than any one man's opinion, be he never so
acute. The law is reason and wisdom itself, free from all perturbation,
not subject to be moved with choler, ambition, hate, or acceptances
of persons. Entreaties nor threats cannot make to bow nor bend; on
the contrary, a man, though endued with reason, suffers himself to be

lead and transported with anger, desire of revenge, and other passions which perplex him in such sort that he loses his understanding, because being composed of reason and disordered affections, he cannot so contain himself but sometimes his passions become his master. Accordingly we see that Valentinian, a good emperor, permits those of the empire to have two wives at once, because he was misled by that impure affection. Because Cambyses, the son of Cyrus, became enamored of his own sister, he would therefore have marriages between brother and sister be approved and held lawful; Cubades, king of the Persians, prohibits the punishment of adulterers; we must look for such laws every day if we will have the law subject to the king. To come to our purpose, the law is an understanding mind, or rather an obstacle of many understandings; the mind being the seal of all the intelligent faculties is (if I may so term it) a parcel of divinity, insomuch as he who obeys the law seems to obey God and receive Him for arbitrator of the matters in controversy.

But, on the contrary, insomuch as man is composed of this divine understanding and of a number of unruly passions, so losing himself in that brutishness as he becomes void of reason, and being in that condition he is no longer a man but a beast; he then who desires rather to obey the king than the law seems to prefer the commandment of a beast before that of God. And furthermore, though Aristotle were the tutor of Alexander, yet he confesses that the Divinity cannot so properly be compared to anything of this life as to the ancient laws of well-governed states. He who prefers the commonwealth applies himself to God's ordinances, but he who leans to the king's fancies instead of law prefers brutish sensuality before well-ordered discretion. To which also the prophets seem to have respect who in some places describe these great empires under the representation of ravening beasts. But to go on, is not he a very beast who had rather have for his guide a blind and mad man than he who sees both with the eyes of the body and mind, a beast rather than God. Whence it comes that

though kings, as says Aristotle, for a while, at the first commanded
without restraint of laws, yet presently after, civilized people reduced
them to a lawful condition by binding them to keep and observe the
laws, and for this unruly absolute authority, it remained only amongst
those who commanded over barbarous nations. He says afterwards
that this absolute power was the next degree to plain tyranny, and he
had absolutely called it tyranny had not these beasts, like barbarians,
willingly subjected themselves unto it. But it will be replied that it is
unworthy the majesty of kings to have their wills bridled by laws. But
I will say that nothing is more royal than to have our unruly desires
ruled by good laws. It is much pity to be restrained from that which
we would do; it is much more worse to will that which we should not
do, but it is the worst of all to do that which the laws forbid.

I hear, methinks, a certain furious tribune of the people who opposed the passing of a law that was made against the excess which
then reigned in Rome, saying, "My masters, you are bridled, you are
idle and fettered with the rude bonds of servitude, your liberty is lost,
a law is laid on you that commands you to be moderate: to what
purpose is it to say you are free, since you may not live in what excess
of pleasure you like?" This is the very complaint of many kings at this
day, and of their minions and flatterers. The royal majesty is abolished
if they may not turn the kingdom topsy-turvy at their pleasure. Kings
may go and shake their ears if laws must be observed. Peradventure,
it is a miserable thing to live if a madman may not be suffered to kill
himself when he will, for what else do those things which violate and
abolish laws, without which, neither empires, no, nor the very societies of freebooters can at all subsist?

Let us then reject these detestable, faithless, and impious vanities
of the court-marmosites, which make kings gods, and receive their
sayings as oracles, and which is worse are so shameless to persuade
kings that nothing is just or equitable of itself, but takes its true form
of justice or injustice, according as it pleases the king to ordain, as if

he were some god which could never err nor sin at all. Certainly, all that which God wills is just, and therefore, suppose it is God's will, but that must be just with the king's will before it is his will. For it is not just because the king has appointed it, but that king is just which appoints that to be held for just, which is so of itself.

We will not then say as Anaxarchus did to Alexander, much perplexed for the death of his friend Clitus, whom he had killed with his own hands, to wit, that Themis, the goddess of Justice, sits by kings' sides, as she does by Jupiter's, to approve and confirm whatsoever to them shall seem good; but rather, she sits as president over kingdoms, to severely chastise those kings who wrong or violate the majesty of the laws. We can nowise approve that saying of Thrasimacus the Chaldonian that the profit and pleasure of princes is the rule by which all laws are defined, but rather that right must limit the profit of princes and the laws restrain their pleasures. And instead of approving that which that villainous woman said to Caracalla, that whatsoever he desired was allowed him, we will maintain that nothing is lawful but what the law permits. And absolutely rejecting that detestable opinion of the same Caracalla, that princes give laws to others, but received none from any, we will say that in all kingdoms well established, the king receives the laws from the people, the which he ought carefully to consider and maintain, and whatsoever, either by force or fraud he does in prejudice of them must always be reputed unjust.

VII. KINGS RECEIVE LAWS FROM THE PEOPLE

These may be sufficiently verified by examples. Before there was a king in Israel, God by Moses prescribed to him both sacred and civil ordinances which he should have perpetually before his eyes, but after Saul was elected and established by the people, Samuel delivered it to him written, to the end he might carefully observe it; neither were the succeeding kings received before they had sworn to keep those ordinances. The ceremony was this: that together with the setting of the crown on the king's head, they delivered into his hands the Book of the Testimony, which some understand to be the right of the people of the land, others, the law of God according to which he ought to govern the people. Cyrus, acknowledging himself conservator of his country's laws, obliges himself to oppose any man who would offer to infringe them, and at his inauguration ties himself to observe them, although some flatterers tickled the ears of his son Cambyses that all things were lawful for him.

The kings of Sparta, whom Aristotle calls lawful princes, did every month renew their oaths, promising in the hands of the ephori, procures for the kingdom, to rule according to those laws which they had from Lycurgus. Hereupon, it being asked Archidamus, the son of Zeuxidamus, who were the governors of Sparta, he answered, "The laws, and the lawful magistrates." And lest the laws might grow into contempt, these people bragged that they received them from heaven and that they were inspired from above, to the end that men might believe that their determinations were from God, and not from man. The kings of Egypt did in nothing vary from the tenor of the laws, and confessed that their principal felicity consisted in the obedience they yielded to them. Romulus, at the institution of the Roman kingdom, made this agreement with senators: the people should make laws, and he would take both for himself and others to see them observed and kept. Antiochus, the third of that name, king of Asia, wrote unto all the cities of his kingdom that if in the letters sent unto them in his name there were anything found repugnant to the laws, they should believe they were no act of the king's and therefore yield no obedience unto them. Now, although some citizens say that by decree of senate the emperor Augustus was declared to be exempt from obedience to laws, yet notwithstanding, Theodosius and all the other good and reasonable emperors have professed that they were bound to the laws, lest what had been extorted by violence might be acknowledged and received instead of law. And for Augustus Caesar, insomuch as the Roman commonwealth was enthralled by his power and violence, she could say nothing freely but that she had lost her freedom. And because they dare not call Augustus a tyrant, the senate said he was exempt from all obedience to the laws, which was in effect as much as if they plainly should have said the emperor was an outlaw. The same right has ever been of force in all well-governed states and kingdoms of Christendom.

For neither the emperor, the king of France, nor the kings of Spain, England, Poland, Hungary, and all other lawful princes, as the archdukes of Austria, dukes of Brabante, earls of Flanders and Holland, nor other princes, are not admitted to the government of their estates before they have promised to the electors, peers, palatines, lords, barons, and governors, that they will render to everyone right according to the laws of the country, yea, so strictly that they cannot alter or innovate anything contrary to the privileges of the countries without the consent of the towns and provinces; if they do it, they are no less guilty of rebellion against the laws than the people are in their kind if they refuse obedience when they command according to law. Briefly, lawful princes receive the laws from the people as well as the crown, in lieu of honor, and the scepter, in lieu of power, which they are bound to keep and maintain, and therein reposes their chiefest glory.

VIII. IF THE PRINCE MAY MAKE NEW LAWS

What then? Shall it not be lawful for a prince to make new laws and abrogate the old? Seeing it belongs to the king, not only to advise that nothing be done neither against, nor to defraud the laws, but also that nothing be wanting to them, nor anything too much in them, briefly, that neither age nor lapse of time do abolish or entomb them, if there be anything to abridge, to be added or taken away from them, it is his duty to assemble the estates, and to demand their advice and resolution, without presuming to publish anything before the whole have been first duly examined and approved by them; after the law is once enacted and published, there is no more dispute to be made about it, all men owe obedience to it, and the prince in the first place, to teach other men their duty; and since all men are easier led by example than by precepts, the prince must necessarily express his willingness to observe the laws, or else by what equity can he require obedience in his subjects, to that which he himself condemns?

For the difference which is between kings and subjects ought not to consist in impunity but in equity and justice. And therefore, although Augustus was esteemed to be exempt by the decree of the senate, notwithstanding, reproving of a young man who had broken the Julian law concerning adultery, he boldly replied to Augustus that he himself had transgressed the same law which condemns adulterers. The emperor acknowledged his fault and for grief forbore too late. So convenient a thing it is in nature to practice by example that which we would teach by precept.

The lawgiver Solon was wont to compare laws to money, for they maintain human societies as money preserves traffic; neither improperly, then, if the king may not lawfully, or at the least heretofore could not, menace or embase good money without the consent of the commonwealth, much more less can he have power to make and unmake laws, without the which, neither kings, nor subjects can cohabit in security, but must be forced to live brutishly in caves and deserts like wild beasts; wherefore also the emperor of Germany, esteeming it needful to make some law for the good of the empire: first he demands the advice of the estates. If it be there approved, the princes, barons, and deputies of the towns sign it, and then the law is satisfied, for he solemnly swears to keep the laws already made and to introduce no new ones without a general consent.

There is a law in Polonia, which has been renewed in the year 1454, and also in the year 1538, and by this it is decreed that no new laws shall be made but by a common consent, nor nowhere else but in the general assembly of the estates. For the kingdom of France, where the kings are thought to have greater authority than in other places, anciently all laws were only made in the assembly of the estates, or in the ambulatory parliament. But since this parliament has been sedentary, the king's edicts are not received as authentic before the parliament has approved them, whereas on the contrary, the decrees of this parliament where the law is defective have commonly the power and effect of law. In the kingdoms of England, Spain, Hungary, and others, they yet enjoy in some sort their ancient privileges.

For if the welfare of the kingdom depends on the observation of the laws, and the laws are enthralled to the pleasure of one man, is it not most certain that there can be no permanent stability in that government? Must it not then necessarily come to pass that if the king (as some have been) be infected with lunacy, either continually or by intervals, that the whole state fall inevitably to ruin? But if the laws be superior to the king, as we have already proved, and that the king be tied in the same respect of obedience to the laws as the servant is to his master, who will be so senseless, who will not rather obey the law than the king or will not readily yield his best assistance against those who seek to violate or infringe them? Now seeing that the king is not lord over the laws, let us examine how far his power may be justly extended in other things.

IX. WHETHER THE PRINCE HAVE POWER OF LIFE AND DEATH OVER HIS SUBJECTS

The minions of the court hold it for an undeniable maxim that princes have the same power of life and death over their subjects as ancient masters had over their slaves, and with these false imaginations have so bewitched princes that many, although they put not in use with much rigor this imaginary right, yet they imagine that they may lawfully do it, and in how much they desist from the practice thereof, insomuch that they quit and relinquish their right and due.

But we affirm on the contrary that the prince is but as the minister and executor of the law, and may only unsheathe the sword against those whom the law has condemned, and if he do otherwise, he is no more a king but a tyrant; no longer a judge, but a malefactor, and instead of that honorable title of conservator, he shall be justly branded with that foul term of violator of the law and equity.

We must here first of all take into our consideration the foundation on which this our disputation is built, which we have resolved into this head, that kings are ordained for the benefit and profit of the public state; this being granted, the question is soon discussed. For who will believe that men sought and desired a king who upon any sudden motion might at his pleasure cut their throats, or which in choler or revenge might, when he would, take their heads from their shoulders? Briefly, who (as the wise man says) carried death at his tongue's end, we must not think so idly.

There is no man so vain who would willingly that his welfare should depend on another's pleasure. Nay, with much difficulty will any man trust his life in the hands of a friend or a brother, much less of a stranger, be he never so worthy. Seeing that envy, hate, rage did so far transport Athanas and Ajax beyond the bounds of reason that the one killed his children, the other failing to effect his desire in the same kind against his friends and companions turned his fury and murderous intent, and acted the same revenge upon himself. Now it being natural to every man to love himself and to seek the preservation of his own life, in what assurance, I pray you, would any man rest to have a sword continually hanging over his head by a small thread, with the point towards him? Would any mirth or jollity relish in such a continual affright? Can you possibly make choice of a more slender thread than to expose your life and welfare into the hands and power of a man so mutable, who changes with every puff of wind, briefly, who almost a thousand times a day, shakes off the restraint of reason and discretion, and yields himself slave to his own unruly and disordered passions. Can there be hoped or imagined any profit or advantage so great or so worthy which might equalize or counterpoise this fear or this danger? Let us conclude then, that it is against delinquents only, whom the mouth of the law has condemned, that kings may draw forth the sword of their authority.

X. IF THE KING MAY PARDON THOSE THE LAW CONDEMNS

B ut, because life is a thing precious and to be favored, peradventure it will be demanded whether the king may not pardon and absolve those whom the law has condemned? I answer, no. Otherwise this cruel pity would maintain thieves, robbers, murderers, ravishers, poisoners, sorcerers, and other plagues of mankind, as we may read tyrants have done heretofore in many places, and to our woeful experience, we may yet see at this present time, and therefore, the stopping of law in this kind will, by impunity, much increase the number of offenders, so that he who received the sword of authority from the law, to pardon offenses, will arm offenders therewith against the laws and put himself the wolf into the fold, which he ought to have warranted from their ravenous outrage.

But forsomuch that it may chance in some occasions that the law being mute may have need of a speaking law, and that the king being in some cases the aptest expositor, taking for the rule of his actions equity and reason, which as the soul of the soul may so clear the intention thereof, as where the offense is rather committed against the words than the intendment of the law, he may free the innocent offender from the guilt thereof, because a just and equitable exposition of the law may in all good reason be taken for law itself as nearest concurring with the intention of the lawmakers. Notwithstanding, lest passion should prepossess the place of reason, kings should in this fashion themselves to the ordinary practice of the emperor Severus, not to determine absolutely anything before it were maturely discussed by upright and discreet men in that faculty.

And so the king may rigorously punish the murderer, and yet, notwithstanding, pardon him, which casually and without any such purpose kills one. He may put to death the thief, and yet pardon that man who in his own defense kills him that would have robbed him. Briefly, in all other occurrences, he may distinguish, as being established arbitrator and neuter, chance-medley from malice, forethought a good purpose from the rigor of the law, without favoring at any time malice or treason. Neither can the right omission of this duty gain to him any true esteem of merciful men, for certainly that shepherd is much more pitiful who kills the wolf than he who lets him escape; the clemency of that king is more commendable who commits the malefactor to the hangman than he who delivers him, by putting to death the murderer many innocents are delivered from danger, whereas by suffering him to escape, both he and others through hope of the like impunity are made more audacious to perpetrate further mischief so that the immediate act of saving one delinquent, arms many hands to murder divers innocents. There is, therefore, both truly mildness in putting to death some, and as certainly cruelty in pardoning of others. Therefore, as it is permitted the king, being as it were guardian of the law, in some cases to interpret the words thereof, so in all well ordered kingdoms it is enjoined the council of state and their duty obliges them to examine the king's interpretation, and to moderate both his severity and facility. If through the corruption and weakness of men this have not been so really and thoroughly observed as it ought, yet notwithstanding the right always remains entire, and there wants only integrity and courage in the parties to make it effectual.

But not to heap up too many examples in a matter so manifestly clear, it has been in this manner practiced in the realm of France. For we have there oftentimes seen those put to death to whom the king had granted his charter of pardon, and those pardoned whom he commanded should be put to death, and sometimes offenses committed in the king's presence remitted because there was no other witness but himself, the which happened in the time of Henry II to a certain stranger who was accused by the king himself of a grievous offence. If an offender by the intercession of friends have his pardon granted by the king, the chancellor upon sufficient cause may cancel it. If the chancellor connive, yet must the criminal present it before the judges, who ought not only carefully to consider whether the pardon were gotten by surreptitious or indirect means, but also if it be legal and in due form. Neither can the delinquent who has obtained his charter of pardon make use of it until first he appeal in public court bare-headed, and on his knees plead it, submitting himself prisoner until the judges have maturely weighed and considered the reasons that induced the king to grant him his pardon. If they be found insufficient, the offender must suffer the punishment of the law, as if the king had not granted him any pardon. But if his pardon be allowed, he ought not so much to thank the king as the equity of the law which saved his life. The manner of these proceedings was excellently ordained, both to contain the king within the limits of equity, lest being armed with public authority he should seek to revenge his own particular spleen or out of fancy or partiality remit the wrongs and outrages committed against the public safety, as partly also to restrain an opinion in the subject that anything could be obtained of the king which might prejudice the laws. If these things have been ill observed in our times, notwithstanding that which we have formerly said remains always certain: that it is the laws which have power over the lives and deaths of the inhabitants of a kingdom, and not the king, who is but administrator and conservator of the laws.

XI. SUBJECTS ARE THE KING'S BRETHREN, AND NOT HIS SLAVES

For truly neither are the subjects, as it is commonly said, the king's slaves or bondmen, being neither prisoners taken in the wars, nor bought for money. But as considered in one entire body they are lords, as we have formerly proved; so each of them in particular ought to be held as the king's brothers and kinsmen. And to the end that we think not this strange, let us hear what God Himself says when He prescribes a law to kings: that they lift not their heart above their brethren from amongst whom they were chosen (Deut. 17:20), whereupon Bartolus, a famous lawyer, who lived in an age that bred many tyrants, did yet draw this conclusion from that law that subjects were to be held and used in the quality and condition of the king's brethren, and not of his slaves. Also king David was not ashamed to call his subjects his brethren. The ancient kings were called Abimelech, a Hebrew word which signifies, "my father the king." The almighty and all good God, of whose great gentleness and mercy we are daily partakers, and very seldom feel His severity, although we justly deserve it, yet is it always mercifully mixed with compassion, whereby He teaches princes, His lieutenants, that subjects ought rather to be held in obedience by love than by fear.

But, lest they should except against me as if I sought to entrench too much upon the royal authority, I verily believe it is so much the greater by how much it is likely to be of longer continuance. For, says one, servile fear is a bad guardian, for that authority we desire should continue; for those in subjection hate those they fear, and whom we hate, we naturally wish their destruction. On the contrary, there is nothing more proper to maintain their authority than the affection of their subjects, on whose love they may safely and with most security lay the foundation of their greatness. And therefore that prince who governs his subjects as brethren may confidently assure himself to live securely in the midst of dangers, whereas he who uses them like slaves must needs live in much anxiety and fear, and may well be resembled to the condition of that master who remains alone in some desert in the midst of a great troop of slaves; for look how many slaves any has, he must make account of so many enemies, which almost all tyrants who have been killed by their subjects have experienced, whereas on the contrary the subjects of good kings are ever as solicitously careful of their safety as of their own welfare.

To this may have reference that which is read in divers places of Aristotle, and was said by Agasicles, king of Sparta, That kings command as fathers over their children, and tyrants as masters over their slaves, which we must take in the same sense that the civilian Martianus does, to wit, that paternal authority consists in piety and not in rigor; for that which was practiced amongst the men of the acorn age, that fathers might sell and put to death their children at their pleasure, has no authority amongst Christians, yea, the very pagans who had any humanity would not permit it to be practiced on their slaves. Therefore, then, the father has no power over the son's life before first the law have determined it, otherwise he offends the law: Cornelius against privy murderers, and by the law Pompeius against parricides, the father is no less guilty who kills the son than the son who murders the father. For the same occasion the emperor Adrian banished into an island, which was the usual punishment for notorious offenders, a father who had slain his son, of whom he had entertained a jealous opinion for his mother-in-law. Concerning servants or slaves, we are admonished in holy writ to use them like brethren, and by human constitutions as hirelings or mercenaries.

By the civil law of the Egyptians and Romans, and by the constitutions of the Antonines, the master is as well liable to punishment who has killed his own slave as he who killed another man's. In like manner the law delivers from the power of the master, the slave whom in his sickness he has altogether neglected or has not afforded convenient food, and the enfranchised slave whose condition was somewhat better, might for any apparent injury bring his action against his patron. Now, seeing there is so great difference between slaves and lawful children, between lords and fathers, and, notwithstanding heretofore, it was not permitted amongst the heathen to use their slaves cruelly, what shall we say, pray you, of that father of the people, who cries out tragically with Atreus, I will devour my children? In what esteem shall we hold that prince who takes such pleasure in the massacre of his subjects (condemned without being ever heard), that he dispatched many thousand of them in one day, and yet is not glutted with blood? Briefly, who, after the example of Caligula (surnamed the Phaeton of the world) wishes that all his people had but one head that he might cut it off at one blow? Shall it not be lawful to implore the assistance of the law against such furious madness and to pull from such a tyrant the sword which he received to maintain the law, and defend the good, when it is drawn by him only for rapine, and ruin?

XII. WHETHER THE PEOPLE'S GOODS BELONG TO THE KING

B ut to proceed, let us now see whether the king, whom we have already proved has not power over the lives of his subjects, is not at the least lord over their goods. In these days there is no language more common in the courts of princes than of those who say all is the king's. Whereby it follows that in exacting anything from his subjects he takes but his own, and in that which he leaves them he expresses the care he has that they should not be altogether destitute of means to maintain themselves, and this opinion has gained so much power in the minds of some princes that they are not ashamed to say that the pains, sweat, and industry of their subjects is the proper revenue, as if their miserable subjects only kept beasts to till the earth for their insolent master's profit and luxury. And indeed, the practice at this day is just in this manner, although in all right and equity it ought to be contrary. Now we must always remember that kings were created for the good and profit of the people, and that these (as Aristotle says) who endeavor and seek the commodity of the people are truly kings, whereas those who make their own private ends and pleasures the only butt and aim of their desires are truly tyrants.

It being then so that everyone loves that which is his own, yea, that many covet that which belongs to other men, is it anything probable that men should seek a master to give him frankly all that they had long labored for and gained with the sweat of their brows? May we not rather imagine that they chose such a man on whose integrity they relied for the administering of justice equally both to the poor and rich, and who would not assume all to himself, but rather maintain everyone in the fruition of his own goods? Or who, like an unprofitable drone, should suck the fruit of other men's labors, but rather preserve the house for those whose industry justly deserved it? Briefly, who, instead of extorting from the true owners their goods would see them defended from all ravening oppressors? What, I pray you matters it, says the poor country man, whether the king or the enemy make havoc of my goods, since through the spoil thereof I and my poor family die for hunger? What imports it whether a stranger or home-bred caterpillar ruin my estate, and bring my poor fortune to extreme beggary? Whether a foreign soldier, or a sycophant courtier, by force or fraud, make me alike miserable? Why shall he be accounted a barbarous enemy if you be a friendly patriot? Why he a tyrant if you be king? Yea, certainly by how much parricide is greater than manslaughter, by so much the wickedness of a king exceeds in mischief the violence of an enemy.

If then, therefore, in the creation of kings, men gave not their own proper goods unto them, but only recommended them to their protection; by what other right then but that of freebooters can they challenge the property of other men's goods to themselves? Wherefore the kings of Egypt were not (according to law) at the first the lords of particular men's estates, but only then when they were sold unto them for corn, and yet may there well be question made of the validity of that contract. Ahab, king of Israel, could not compel Naboth to sell him his vineyard, but rather if he had been willing, the law of God would not permit it. The Roman emperors who had an unreasonable power could neither by right have done it. At this day there is with much difficulty any kingdom to be found where the meanest subject may not suit the king, and where many times the king is not cast in the suit, which succeeding, he must as well as others satisfy the judgment. And to this is not contrary, although at the first view it seem so, that which some of their most familiars have written of the emperors. That by the civil law all things were the king's, and that Caesar was absolute lord of all things, they themselves expound this their opinion in this manner: that the dominion of all things belongs to the king, and the propriety to particular persons, insomuch as the one possesses all by the right of commanding, the other by the law of inheritance. We know that it is a common saying amongst the civilians that if any make claim to a house or a ship, it follows not therefore that he can extend his right to all the furniture or cargo. And therefore a king may challenge and gain right to the kingdom of Germany, France, and England, and yet, notwithstanding, he may not lawfully take any honest man's estate from him but by a manifest injustice, seeing that they are things diverse, and by law distinguished to be possessors of the whole, and of all the particular parts.

XIII. WHETHER THE KING BE THE OWNER OF THE KINGDOM

B ut the king, is he not lord proprietor of the public revenue? We must handle this point somewhat more exactly than we did the former. In the first place, we must consider that the revenue of the public exchequer is one thing, and the proper patrimony of the prince another; of different nature are the goods of the emperor, king, or prince, to those of Antonius, Henry, or Phillip; those are properly the king's, which he enjoys as king, those are Antonius' his which he possesses, as in the right of Antonius, the former he received from the people, the latter from those of his blood, as inheritor to them.

This distinction is frequent in the books of the civil law, where there is a difference ever made between the patrimony of the empire, and that of the emperor: the treasury of Caesar is one thing, and the exchequer of the commonwealth another, and both the one and the other have their several procurers, there being diverse dispensers of the sacred and public distributions, and of the particular and private expenses, insomuch as he who as emperor is preferred before a private man in a grant by deed or charter may also sometime as Antonius give place to an inferior person.

In like manner in the empire of Germany the revenue of Ferdinand of Austria is one thing, and the revenue of the Emperor Ferdinand is another: the empire and the emperor have their several treasures, as also there is difference in the inheritances which the princes derive from the houses of their ancestors, and those which are annexed to the electoral dignities. Yea, amongst the Turks themselves, Selimus, his gardens and patrimonial lands, are distinguished from those of the public, the one serving for the provision of the Sultan's table, the other employed only about the Turkish affairs of state. There be, notwithstanding kingdoms, as the French and English and others in which the king has no particular patrimony, but only the public which he received from the people; there this former distinction has no place. For the goods which belong to the prince as a private person there is no question; he is absolute owner of them as other particular persons are, and may by the civil law sell, engage, or dispose of them at his pleasure. But for the goods of the kingdom, which in some places are commonly called the demesnes, the kings may not be esteemed nor called in any sort whatsoever absolute lords proprietors of them.

For what if a man for the flocks' sake have made you shepherd, does it follow that you hast liberty to slay, pill, sell, and transport the sheep at thy pleasure? Although the people have established you judge or governor of a city, or of some province, hast you therefore power to alienate, sell, or play away that city or province? And seeing that in alienating or passing away a province, the people also are sold, have they raised you to that authority to the end you should separate them from the rest, or that you should prostitute and make them slaves to whom you please? Furthermore, I demand if the royal dignity be a patrimony, or an office? If it be an office, what community has it with any propriety? If it be a patrimony, is it not such a one that at least the paramount propriety remains still in the people who were the donors? Briefly, if the revenue of the exchequer or the demesnes of the kingdom be called the dowry of the commonwealth, and by good right and such a dowry whose dismembering or wasting brings with it the ruin of the public state, the kingdom and the king, by what law shall it be lawful to alienate this dowry? Let the emperor Wenceslaus be infatuated, the French King Charles the Sixth lunatic, and give or sell the kingdom or part of it to the English, let Malcolm, King of the Scots, lavishly dissipate the demesnes and consume the public treasure, what follows for all this? Those who choose the king to withstand the invasions of foreign enemies, shall they through his madness and negligence be made the slaves of strangers? And those means and wealth, which would have secured them in the fruition of their own estates and fortunes, shall they, by the election of such a king, be exposed to the prey and rapine of all comers? And that which particular persons have saved from their own necessities, and from those under their tutorship and government (as it happened in Scotland) to endue the commonwealth with it, shall it be devoured by some pander or broker for unclean pleasures?

But if, as we have often said, that kings were constituted for the people's use, what shall that use be if it be perverted into abuse? What good can so much mischief and inconvenience bring? What profit can come of such eminent and irreparable damages and dangers? If, I say, in seeking to purchase my own liberty and welfare, I engage myself into an absolute thralldom, and willingly subject myself to another's yoke, and become a fettered slave to another man's unruly desires, therefore, as it is imprinted in all of us by nature, so also has it by a long custom been approved by all nations that it is not lawful for the king by the counsel of his own fancy and pleasure, to diminish or waste the public revenue; and those who have run a contrary course have even lost that happy name of a king, and stood branded with the infamous title of a tyrant.

I confess that when kings were instituted, there was of necessity means to be assigned for them, as well to maintain their royal dignity, as to furnish the expense of their train and officers. Civility, and the welfare of the public state, seem to require it, for it was the duty of a king to establish judges, in all places, who should receive no presents, nor sell justice: and also to have power ready to assist the execution of their ordinances, and to secure the ways from dangers, that commerce might be open, and free, etc. If there were likelihood of wars, to fortify and put garrisons into the frontier places, and to hold an army in the field, and to keep his magazines well stored with ammunition. It is commonly said, that peace cannot be well maintained without provision for wars, nor wars managed without men, nor men kept in discipline without pay, nor money got without subsidies and tributes.

To discharge therefore the burden of the state in time of peace was the demesne appointed, and in time of wars the tributes and imports, yet so as if any extraordinary necessity required it, money might be raised by subsidies or other fitting means. The final intendment of all was ever the public utility, insomuch as he who converts any of these public revenues to his own private purposes, much more he who misspends them in any unworthy or loose occasions, no way merits the name of a king, for the prince (says the apostle) is the minister of God for the good of the people, and for that cause is tribute paid unto them.

This is the true original cause of the customs and imposts of the Romans, that those rich merchandises which were brought from the Indies, Arabia, Ethiopia, might be secured in their passage by land from thieves and robbers, and in their transportation by sea from pirates, insomuch as for their security, the commonwealth maintained a navy at sea. In this rank we must put the custom which was paid in the Red Sea, and other imposts of gates, bridges, and passages, for the securing of the great roadways (therefore called the Pretorian Consular, and the king's highways) from the spoil of thieves and freebooters. The care also of the reparation of bridges was referred to commissaries deputed by the king, as appears by the ordinance of Lewis the Courteous, concerning the twelve bridges over the river

Seine, commanding also boats to be in readiness to ferry over passengers, etc.

For the tax laid upon salt there was none in use in those times, the most of the salt-pits being enjoyed by private persons, because it seemed that that which nature out of her own bounty presented unto men ought no more to be enhanced by sale than either the light, the air, or the water. As a certain king called Lycurgus in the lesser Asia began to lay some impositions upon the salt-pits there, nature, as it were, impatiently bearing such a restraint of her liberality, the springs are said to have dried up suddenly. Yet certain marmosets of the court would persuade us at this day (as Juvenal complained in his time) that the sea affords nothing of worth, or good, which falls not within the compass of the king's prerogative.

He who first brought this taxation into Rome was the Censor Livius, who therefore gained the surname of Salter; neither was it done but in the commonwealth's extreme necessity. And in France King Philip the Long for the same reason obtained of the estates the imposition upon salt for five years only. What turmoils and troubles the continuance thereof has bred every man knows. To be brief, all tributes were imposed and continued for the provision of means and stipends for the men of war, so as to make a province stipendiary or tributary was esteemed the same with military.

Behold wherefore Solomon exacted tributes, to wit, to fortify the towns, and to erect and furnish a public magazine, which being accomplished the people required of Rehoboam to be freed from that burden. The Turks call the tribute of the provinces the sacred blood of the people, and account it a most wicked crime to employ it in anything but the defense of the people. Wherefore, by the same reason, all that which the king conquers in war belongs to the people and not to the king, because the people bore the charges of the war, as that which is gained by a factor accrues to the account of his master. Yea, and what advantage he gains by marriage, if it belongs simply and absolutely to his wife, that is acquired also to the kingdom, forsomuch as it is to be presumed that he gained not that preferment in marriage in quality of Philip or Charles, but as he was king. On the contrary, in like manner, the queens have interest of endowment in the estates which their husbands gained and enjoyed before they attained the crown, and have no title to that which is gotten after they are created kings, because that is judged as the acquisition of the common purse, and has no proper reference to the king's private estate, which was so determined in France, betwixt Philip of Valois and his wife Jean of Burgundy. But to the end that there be no money drawn from the people to be employed in private designs, and for particular ends and purposes, the emperor swears not to impose any taxes or tributes whatsoever, but by the authority of the estates of the empire. As much do the kings of Polonia, Hungary, and Denmark promise: the English in like manner enjoy the same unto this day by the laws of Henry the Third and Edward the First.

The French kings in former times imposed no taxes but in the assemblies, and with the consent of the three estates; from thence sprung the law of Philip of Valois that the people should not have any tribute laid on them but in urgent necessity and with the consent of the estates. Yea, and anciently, after these moneys were collected, they were locked in coffers through every diocese and recommended to the special care of selected men (who are the same who at this day are called esleus), to the end that they should pay the soldiers enrolled within the towns of their dioceses, the which was in use in other countries, as namely in Flanders and other neighboring provinces. At this day, though many corruptions have crept in, yet without the consent and confirmation of the parliament, no exactions may be collected; notwithstanding, there are some provinces which are not bound to anything without the approbation of the estates of the country, as Languedoke, Brittany, Province, Daulphiny, and some others. Finally, all the provinces of the low countries have the same privileges, lest the exchequer devour all, like the spleen which exhales the spirits from the other members of the body. In all places they have confined the exchequer within its proper bounds and limits.

Seeing then it is most certain that what has been ordinarily and extraordinarily assigned to kings, to wit, tributes, taxes, and all the demesnes which comprehend all customs, both importations and exportations, forfeitures, amercements, royal escheats, confiscations, and other dues of the same nature were consigned into their hands for the maintenance and defense of the people and the state of the kingdom, insomuch as if the sinews be cut, the people must needs fall to decay, and in demolishing these foundations the kingdom will come to utter ruin; it necessarily follows that he who lays impositions on the people only to oppress them, and by the public detriment seeks private profit, and with their own sword kills his subjects, he truly is unworthy the name of a king, whereas contrarily, a true king, as he is a careful manager of the public affairs, so is he a ready protector of the common welfare, and not a lord in propriety of the commonwealth, having as little authority to alienate or dissipate the demesnes or public revenue as the kingdom itself. And if he misgovern the state, seeing it imports the commonwealth that everyone make use of his own talent, it is much more requisite for the public good that he who has the managing of it carry himself as he ought.

And therefore, if a prodigal lord by the authority of justice be committed to the tuition of his kinsmen and friends and compelled to suffer his revenues and means to be ordered and disposed of by others, by much more reason may those who have interest in the affairs of state and whose duty obliges them thereto take all the administration and government of the state out of the hands of him who either negligently executes his place or ruins the commonwealth, if after admonition he endeavors not to perform his duty. And forsomuch as it is easily to be proved without searching into those elder times that in all lawful dominions the king cannot be held lord in propriety of the demesnes, whereof we have an apt representation in the person of Ephron king of the Hittites, who dared not to sell the field to Abraham without the consent of the people. This right is at this day practiced in public states: the emperor of Germany before his coronation solemnly swears that he will neither alienate, dismember, nor engage any of the rights or members of the empire. And if he recover or conquer anything with the arms and means of the public, it shall be gained to the empire, and not to himself. Wherefore when Charles the Fourth promised each of the electors a hundred thousand crowns to choose his son Wenceslaus emperor, and having not ready money to deliver them, he mortgaged customs, taxes, tributes, and certain towns unto them, which were the proper appurtenances of the empire, whereon followed much and vehement contestation, most men holding this engagement void. And questionless it had been so declared, but for the profit that those reaped thereby who ought principally to have maintained and held entire the rights and dignities of the empire. And it followed also that Wenceslaus was justly held incapable of the government of the empire, chiefly because he suffered the rights of the empire over the duchy of Milan to be wrested from him.

There is a law very ancient in the kingdom of Polonia which prohibits the alienating of any of the kingdom's lands, the which also was renewed by King Lewis in the year 1375. In Hungary in A.D. 1221 there was a complaint made to Pope Honorius that King Andrew had engaged the crown lands contrary to his oath. In England was the same by the law of King Edward in the year 1298; likewise in Spain by the ordinance made under Alphonsus, and renewed in the year 1560, in the assembly of the estates at Toledo. These laws were then ratified, although long time before custom had obtained the vigor and effect of law.

Now, for the kingdom of France whereto I longer confine myself, because she may in a sort pass as a pattern to the rest, this right has ever remained there inviolable. It is one of the most ancient laws of the kingdom, and a right born with the kingdom itself, that the demesne may not be alienated, the which law in A.D. 1566 (although but ill deserved) was renewed. There are only two cases excepted, the portions or appanages of the children and brothers of the king, yet with this reservation: that the right of vassalage remains always to the crown in like manner if the condition of war require necessarily an alienation, yet it must be ever with power of redemption. Anciently neither the one nor the other were of validity, but by the commandment of the states; at this day since the parliament has been made sedentary, the parliament of Paris which is the court of the peers and the chamber of accounts and of the treasury must first approve it as the edicts of Charles the Sixth and Ninth do testify. This is a thing so certain that if the ancient kings themselves would endow a church (although that was a work much favored in those days), they were notwithstanding bound to have an allowance of the estates: witness King Childebert, who might not endow the Abbey of Saint Vincent at Paris before he had the French and Neustrians' consent. Clovis the Second and other kings have observed the same. They might neither remit the regalities by granting enfranchisements, nor the nomination of prelates to any church. And if any of them have done it, as Lewis the Second, Philip the Fourth, and Philip surnamed Augustus did in favor of the churches of Senis Auxera, and Nevers, the parliament has declared it void. When the king is anointed at Rheims, he swears to observe this law, and if he infringe it, that act has as much validity with it as if he contracted to sell the empires of the Great Turk, or Sophia of Persia. From this spring the constitutions or ordinances of Philip the Sixth, of John the Second, of Charles the Fifth, Sixth, and Eighth, by which they revoke all alienations made by their predecessors.

In the assembly of the estates at Tours, where King Charles the Eighth was in person, divers alienations made by Lewis the Second were repealed and annihilated, and there was taken away from the heirs of Tancred of Chastel his great minion, divers places which he had given him by his proper authority. This was finally ratified in the last assembly of the estates held at Orleans. Thus much concerning the kingdom's demesne. But to the end that we may yet more clearly perceive that the kingdom is preferred before the king, and that he cannot by his own proper authority diminish the majesty he has received from the people, nor enfranchise or release from his dominion any one of his subjects; nor quit or relinquish the sovereignty of the least part of his kingdom. Charlemagne in former times endeavored to subject the kingdom of France to the German empire, the which the French did courageously oppose by the mouth of a prince of Glasconnie, and if Charlemagne had proceeded in that business, it had come to the trial of the sword. In like manner when any portion of the kingdom was granted to the English, the sovereignty was almost always reserved. And if sometimes they obtained it by force, as at the treaty of Bretigny, by the which King John quitted the sovereignty of Glasconnie and Poytou, that agreement was not kept, neither was he more bound to do it than a tutor or guardian is being prisoner (as he was then), which for his own deliverance should engage the estate of his pupils.

By the power of the same law the parliament of Paris made void the treaty of Conlius, by the which Duke Charles of Burgundy had drawn from the king Amiens and other towns of Picardy. In our days the same parliament declared void the agreement made at Madrid between Francis the First, then prisoner, and Charles the Fifth, concerning the Duchy of Burgundy. But the domain made by Charles the Sixth unto Henry King of England, of the kingdom of France after his decease is a sufficient testimony for this matter and of his madness, if there had been no other proof. But to leave off producing any further testimonies, examples, or reasons, by what right can the king give or sell away the kingdom, or any part of it, seeing it consists of people, and not of earth or walls? And of freemen there can be made no sale, nor traffic, yea, and the patrons themselves cannot compel the enfranchised servants to make their habitations in other places than themselves like, the which is the rather to be allowed in that subjects are neither slaves nor enfranchised servants, but brothers, and not only the king's brethren taken one by one, but also considered in one body, they ought to be esteemed absolute lords and owners of the kingdom.

XIV. WHETHER THE KING BE USUFRUCTOR OF THE KINGDOM

But if the king be not lord in propriety, yet at the least we may esteem him usufructor of the kingdom, and of the demesne, nay, truly we can allow him to have the usufruct for being usufructor, though the propriety remain in the people, yet may he absolutely dispose of the profits and engage them at his pleasure. Now we have already proved that kings of their own authority cannot engage the revenues of the exchequer or the demesne of the kingdom. The usufructor may dispose of the profits to whom, how, and when he pleases. Contrarily, the excessive gifts of princes are ever judged void, his unnecessary expenses are not allowed, his superfluous to be cut off, and that which is expended by him in any other occasion but for the public utility is justly esteemed to be unjustly extorted, and is no less liable to the law Cincea, than the meanest Roman citizen formerly was. In France, the king's gifts are never of force until the chamber of accounts have confirmed them. From hence proceed the postils of the ordinary chamber in giving up of the accounts in the reigns of prodigal kings, *Trop donne: soyt repele*, which is, excessive gifts must be recalled. The judges of this chamber solemnly swear to pass nothing which may prejudice the kingdom or the public state, notwithstanding any letters the king shall write unto them; but they are not always so mindful of this oath as were to be desired.

Furthermore, the law takes no care how a usufructor possesses and governs his revenues, but contrariwise it prescribes unto the king how and to what use he shall employ his. For the ancient kings of France were bound to divide their royal revenues into four parts. The first was implied in the maintaining of the ministers of the church and providing for the poor; the second for the king's table; the third for the wages of his officers and household servants; the last in repairing of bridges, castles, and the royal palaces. And what was remaining was laid up in the treasury to be bestowed on the necessities of the commonwealth. And histories do at large relate the troubles and tumults which happened about the year 1412 in the assembly of the estates at Paris, because Charles the Sixth had wasted all the money that was raised of the revenues and demesne in his own and his minion's loose pleasures, and the expenses of the king's household, which before exceeded not the sum of ninety-four thousand francs, did amount in that miserable estate of the commonwealth to five hundred and forty thousand francs. Now as the demesne was employed in the before-mentioned affairs, so the aids were only for the war, and the taxes assigned for the payment of the men at arms and for no other occasion. In other kingdoms the king has no greater authority, and in divers less, especially in the empire of Germany and in Poland. But we have made choice of the kingdom of France to the end it be not thought this has any special prerogative above others, because there perhaps the commonwealth receives the most detriment. Briefly, as I have before said, the name of a king signifies not an inheritance, nor a propriety, nor a usufruct, but a charge, office, and procuration.

As a bishop is chosen to look to the welfare of the soul, so is the king established to take care of the body, so far forth as it concerns the public good; the one is dispenser of the heavenly treasure, the other of the secular, and what right the one has in the episcopal revenues, the same has the other, and no greater in the kingdom's demesne. If the bishop alien the goods of the bishopric without the consent of the chapter, this alienation is of no value; if the king alien the demesne without the approbation of the estates that is also void; one portion of the ecclesiastical goods ought to be employed in the reparation of the churches; the second in relieving of the poor; the third for the maintenance of the church men; and the fourth for the bishop himself. We have seen before that the king ought to divide into four parts the revenues of the kingdom's demesne. The abuse of these times cannot infringe or annihilate the right. For although some part of the bishops steal from the poor that which they profusely cast away on their panders, and ruin and destroy their lands and woods, the calling of the bishops is not for all that altered. Although some emperors have assumed to themselves an absolute power, that cannot invest them with any further right because no man can be judge in his own cause. What if some Caracalla vaunt he will not want money whilst the sword remains in his custody? The Emperor Adrian will promise on the contrary so to discharge his office of principality that he will always remember that the commonwealth is not his but the people's, which one thing almost distinguishes a king from a tyrant. Neither can that act of Attalus King of Pergamus designing the Roman people for heirs to his kingdom, nor that of Alexander for Egypt, nor Ptolemy for the Cyrenians, bequeathing their kingdoms to the same people, nor Prasutagus King of the Icenians, who left his to Caesar, draw any good consequence of right to those who usurp that which by no just title belongs to them, nay, by how much the intrusion is more violent by so much the equity and justice of the cause is more perspicuous. For what the Romans assumed under the color of right, they would have made no difficulty if that pretext had been wanting to have taken by force. We have seen almost in our days how the Venetians possessed themselves of the kingdom of Cyprus, under pretense of an imaginary adoption, which would have proved ridiculous if it had not been seconded by power and arms, to which also may be not unfitly resembled the pretended donation of Constantine to Pope Sylvester, for that straw of the decretist Gratian was long since consumed and turned to ashes; neither is of more validity the grant which Lewis the Courteous made to Pope Paschal of the city of Rome and part of Italy. Because he gave that which he possessed not, no man opposed it. But when his father Charlemagne would have united and subjected the kingdom of France to the German empire, the French did lawfully oppose it, and if he had persisted in his purpose, they were resolved to have hindered him and defended themselves by arms.

There can be, too, as little advantage alleged that act of Solomon's, whom we read to have delivered twenty towns to Hiram King of Tyre, for he did not give them to him but for the securing of the talents of gold which Hiram had lent him, and they were redeemed at the end of the term, as it appears by the text. Further, the soil was barren and husbanded by the remaining Canaanites. But Solomon, having redeemed it out of the hands of Hiram, delivered it to the Israelites to be inhabited and tilled. Neither serves it to much more purpose to allege that in some kingdoms there is no express agreement between the king and the people; for suppose there be no mention made, yet the law of nature teaches us that kings were not ordained to ruin, but to govern the commonwealths, and that they may not by their proper authority alter or change the rights of the public state, and although they be lords, yet can they challenge it in no other quality than as guardians do in the tuition of their pupils; neither can we account him a lawful lord who deprives the commonwealth of her liberty and sells her as a slave. Briefly, neither can we also allege that some kingdoms are the proper acquisitions of the king himself, insomuch as they were not conquered by their proper means and swords, but by the hands and with the wealth of the public, and there is nothing more agreeable to reason than that which was gained with the joint

difficulties and common danger of the public should not be alienated or disposed of without the consent of the states which represent
the commonwealth, and the necessity of this law is such that it is of
force amongst robbers and freebooters themselves. He who follows
a contrary course must needs ruin human society. And although the
French conquered by force of arms the countries of Germany and
Gaul, yet this before-mentioned right remains still entire.

To conclude, we must needs resolve that kings are neither proprietors nor usufructuaries of the royal patrimony, but only administrators. And being so, they can by no just right attribute to themselves the
propriety, use, or profit of private men's estates, nor with as little reason the public revenues, which are in truth only the commonwealth's.

But before we pass any further, we must here resolve a doubt. The
people of Israel having demanded a king, the Lord said to Samuel:
harken unto the voice of the people; notwithstanding, give them to
understand what shall be the manner of the king who shall reign
over them: "he will take your fields, your vineyards, your olive trees,
to furnish his own occasions, and to enrich his servants," briefly, "he
will make the people slaves" (1 Sam. 8:14). One would hardly believe
in what estimation the courtiers of our times hold this text, when
of all the rest of the Holy Scripture they make but a jest. In this
place the almighty and all good God would manifest to the Israelites their levity, when that they had God Himself even present with
them, who upon all occasions appointed them holy judges and worthy commanders for the wars, would notwithstanding rather subject
themselves to the disordered commandments of a vain mutable man
than to the secure protection of the omnipotent and immutable God.
He declares then unto them in what a slippery estate the king was
placed, and how easily unruly authority fell into disordered violence,
and kingly power was turned into tyrannous willfulness. Seeing the
king that he gave them would by preposterous violence draw the
sword of authority against them and subject the equity of the law to

his own unjust desires, and this mischief which they willfully drew on themselves, they would happily repent of when it would not be so easily remedied. Briefly, this text does not describe the rights of kings, but what right they are accustomed to attribute to themselves, not what by the privilege of their places they may justly do, but what power for the satisfying of their own lusts they unjustly usurp. This will manifestly appear from the seventeenth chapter of Deuteronomy, where God appoints a law for kings. Here says Samuel: "the king will use his subjects like slaves." There God forbids the king "to lift his heart above his brethren," to wit, "over his subjects, whom he ought not to insult over, but to cherish as his kinsmen." "He will make chariots, levy horsemen, and take the goods of private men," says Samuel (1 Sam. 8:11); on the contrary in Deuteronomy, he is exhorted "not to multiply horse-men, nor to heap up gold and silver, nor cause the people to return into Egypt," to wit, into bondage (Deut. 17:16). In the eighth chapter of Samuel we see pictured wicked Ahab, who by pernicious means gets Naboth's vineyard; there, David, who held it not lawful to drink that water which was purchased with the danger of his subjects' lives. Samuel foretells that the king demanded by the Israelites, instead of keeping the laws, would govern all according to his own fancy. On the contrary, God commands that His law should by the priests be delivered into the hands of the king, to copy it out and to have it continually before his eyes. Therefore Samuel, being high priest, gave to Saul the royal law contained in the seventeenth of Deuteronomy written into a book, which certainly had been a frivolous act if the king were permitted to break it at his pleasure. Briefly, it is as much as if Samuel had said: you have asked a king after the manner of other nations, the most of whom have tyrants for their governors: you desire a king to distribute justice equally amongst you, but many of them think all things lawful which their own appetites suggest unto them; in the mean season you willingly shake off the Lord, whose only will is equity and justice in the abstract.

In Herodotus there is a history which plainly expresses how apt the royal government is to degenerate into tyranny, whereof Samuel so exactly forewarns the people. Deioces, much renowned for his justice, was first chosen judge amongst the Medes; presently afterwards, to the end he might the better repress those who would oppose justice, he was chosen king and invested with convenient authority; then he desired a guard, afterwards, a citadel to be built in Ecbatana, the principal city of the kingdom, with color to secure him from conspiracies and machinations of rebels, which being effected, he presently applied himself to revenge the least displeasures which were offered him with the greatest punishments.

Finally, no man might presume to look this king in the face and to laugh or cough in his presence was punished with grievous torments. So dangerous a thing it is to put into the hands of a weak mind (as all men's are by nature) unlimited power. Samuel therefore teaches not in that place that the authority of a king is absolute; on the contrary, he discreetly admonishes the people not to enthrall their liberty under the unnecessary yoke of a weak and unruly master; he does not absolutely exclude the royal authority, but would have it restrained within its own limits; he does not amplify the king's right with an unbridled and licentious liberty, but rather tacitly persuades to put a bit into his mouth. It seems that this advice of Samuel's was very beneficial to the Israelites, for they circumspectly moderated the power of their kings, the which, most nations grown wise, either by the experience of their own or their neighbor's harms, have carefully looked unto, as will plainly appear by that which follows.

We have showed already that in the establishing of the king there were two alliances or covenants contracted: the first between God, the king, and the people, of which we have formerly treated; the second between the king and the people, of which we must now say somewhat. After Saul was established king, the royal law was given him according to which he ought to govern. David made a covenant in Hebron before the Lord, that is to say, taking God for witness with all the ancients of Israel who represented the whole body of the people, and even then he was made king. Joash also by the mouth of Jehoiada the high priest entered into covenant with the whole people of the land in the house of the Lord. And when the crown was set on his head, together with it was the law of the testimony put into his hand which most expounds to be the law of God; likewise Josiah promises to observe and keep the commandments, testimonies, and statutes comprised in the book of the covenant, under which words are contained all which belongs to the duties both of the first and second table of the law of God. In all the before-remembered places of the holy story it is ever said that "a covenant was made with all the people, with all the multitude, with all the elders, with all the men of Judah," to the end that we might know, as it is also fully expressed, that not only the principals of the tribes, but also all the milleniers, centurions, and subaltern magistrates should meet together, each of them in the name, and for their towns and communalties, to covenant and contract with the king. In this assembly was the creating of the king determined of, for it was the people who made the king, and not the king the people.

It is certain, then, that the people by way of stipulation require a performance of covenants. The king promises it. Now the condition of a stipulator is in terms of law more worthy than of a promiser. The people ask the king whether he will govern justly and according to the laws? He promises he will. Then the people answer, and not before, that whilst he governs uprightly they will obey faithfully. The king therefore promises simply and absolutely; the people upon condition, the which failing to be accomplished, the people rest according to equity and reason quit from their promise. In the first covenant or contract there is only an obligation to piety; in the second, to justice, in that the king promises to serve God religiously: in this, to rule the people justly. The most important affairs, and esteemed it a great error, without their advice, to resolve on the occasions of the public state.

If we take into our consideration the condition of the empires, kingdoms, and states of times, there is not any of them worthy of those names where there is not some such covenant or confederacy between the people and the prince. It is not long since that in the empire of Germany the king of the Romans being ready to be crowned emperor was bound to do homage and make oath of fealty to the empire, no more nor less than as the vassal is bound to do to his lord when he is invested with his fee. Although the form of the words which he is to swear have been somewhat altered by the popes, yet, notwithstanding, the substance still remains the same. According to which we know that Charles the Fifth, of the house of Austria, was under certain conditions, chosen emperor, as in the same manner his successors were, the sum of which was that he should keep the laws already made and make no new ones without the consent of the electors, that he should govern the public affairs by the advice of the general estates, nor engage anything that belongs to the empire, and other matters which are particularly recited by the historians. When the emperor is crowned at Aquisgrave, the Archbishop of Cologne requires of him in the first place if he will maintain the church, if he will distribute justice, if he will defend the empire, and protect widows, orphans, and all others worthy of compassion, the which, after he has solemnly sworn before the altar, the princes also who represent the empire are asked if they will not promise the same; neither is the emperor anointed, nor receives the other ornaments of the empire before he has first taken that solemn oath. Whereupon it follows that the emperor is tied absolutely, and the princes of the empire under condition. That the same is observed in the kingdom of Polonia no man will make question who had but seen or heard of the ceremonies and rites wherewith Henry of Anjou was lately chosen and crowned king of that country, and especially then when

the condition of maintaining of the two religions, the reformed and
the Roman, was demanded, the which the lords of the kingdom in
express terms required of him three several times, and he as often
made promise to perform. The same is observed in the kingdoms of
Bohemia, Hungary, and others, the which we omit to relate particularly, to avoid prolixity.

Now this manner of stipulation is not only received in those kingdoms where the right of election is yet entirely observed, but even
in those also which are esteemed to be simply hereditary. When the
king of France is crowned, the bishops of Laon and Beauvois, ecclesiastical peers, ask all the people there present whether they desire
and command that he who is there before them shall be their king,
whereupon he is said even then in the style of the inauguration to
be chosen by the people, and when they have given the sign of con-
senting, then the king swears that he will maintain all the rights,
privileges, and laws of France universally, that he will not alien the
demesne and the other articles which have been yet so changed and
accommodated to bad intentions, as they differ greatly from that
copy which remains in the library of the chapter of Beauvois, according to which it is recorded that King Philip, the first of that name,
took his oath at his coronation; yet notwithstanding they are not
unfitly expressed. Neither is he girded with the sword, nor anointed,
nor crowned by the peers (who at that time wore coronets on their
heads), nor receives the scepter and rod of justice, nor is proclaimed
king before first the people have commanded it; neither do the peers
take their oaths of allegiance before he has first solemnly sworn to
keep the laws carefully.

And those be that he shall not waste the public revenue, that he
shall not of his own proper authority impose any taxes, customs,
or tributes, that he shall not make peace or war, nor determine of
state affairs without the advice of the council of state; briefly, that
he should leave to the parliament, to the states, and to the officers

of the kingdom their authority entire, and all things else which have been usually observed in the kingdom of France. And when he first enters any city or province, he is bound to confirm their privileges and swears to maintain their laws and customs. This is straightly observed in the cities of Tholouse and Rochel, and in the countries of Daulpiny, Province, and Brittany, the which towns and provinces have their particular and express covenants and agreements with the kings, which must needs be void if the condition expressed in the contract be not of force, nor the kings tied to the performance.

There is the form of the oath of the ancient kings of Burgundy, yet extant in these words: "I will protect all men in their rights, according to law and justice." In England, Scotland, Sweden, and Denmark, there is almost the same custom as in France, but in no place there is used a more discreet care in their manner of proceeding than in Spain. For in the kingdom of Arragon, after the finishing of many ceremonies which are used between him which represents the Justitia Major of Arragon, which comprehends the majesty of the commonwealth, seated in a higher seat, and the king, which is to be crowned, who swears fealty, and does his homage, and having read the laws and conditions, to the accomplishment whereof he is sworn.

Finally, the lords of the kingdom use to the king these words in the vulgar language, as is before expressed, "We who are as much worth as you, and have more power than you, choose you king upon these and these conditions, and there is one between you and us, who commands over you." But, lest the king should think he swore only for fashion's sake and to observe an old custom, every third year in full assembly of the estates, the very same words, and in the same manner are repeated unto him. And if under pretext of his royal dignity he become insolent, violating the laws, and neglect his public faith and promise given, then by the privilege of the kingdom he is judged, excommunicated as execrable as Julian the apostate was by the primitive church, which excommunication is esteemed of that validity that instead of praying for the king in their public orations, they pray against him, and the subjects are by the same right acquit from their oath of allegiance, as the vassal is exempted from obedience and obligation by oath to his lord who stands excommunicated, the which hath been determined and confirmed both by act of council and decree of state in the kingdom of Arragon.

In like manner in the kingdom of Castile in full assembly of the estates, the king, being ready to be crowned, is first in the presence of all advertised of his duty, and even then are read the articles discreetly composed for the good of the commonwealth; the king swears he will observe and keep them carefully and faithfully, which being done then the constable takes his oath of allegiance after the princes and deputies for the towns swear each of them in their order, and the same is observed in the kingdoms of Portugal, Leon, and the rest of Spain. The lesser principalities have their institution grounded on the same right. The contracts which the Brabancers and the rest of the Netherlanders, together with those of Austria, Carinthia, and others had with their princes, were always conditional. But especially the Brabancers, to take away all occasion of dispute, have this express condition: which is that in the receiving of their duke there is read in his presence the ancient articles, wherein is comprised that which is requisite for the public good, and thereunto is also added that if he do not exactly and precisely observe them, they may choose what other lord it shall seem good unto them, the which they do in express words protest unto him. He having allowed and accepted of these articles does in that public assembly promise and solemnly swear to keep them, the which was observed in the reception of Philip the Second, king of Spain. Briefly, there is not any man can deny but that there is a contract mutually obligatory between the king and the subjects, which requires the people to obey faithfully and the king to govern lawfully, for the performance whereof the king swears first, and after the people.

I would ask here, wherefore a man does swear, if it be not to declare that what he delivers he sincerely intends from his heart? Can anything be judged more near to the law of nature than to observe that which we approve? Furthermore, what is the reason the king swears first, and at the instance, and required by the people, but to accept a condition either tacit or expressed? Wherefore is there a condition opposed to the contract, if it be not that in failing to perform the condition, the contract, according to law, remains void? And if for want of satisfying the condition by right, the contract is of no force, who shall dare to call that people perjured which refuses to obey a king who makes no account of his promise, which he might and ought to have kept, and willfully breaks those laws which he did swear to observe? On the contrary, may we not rather esteem such a king perfidious, perjured, and unworthy of his place? For if the law free the vassal from his lord who dealt feloniously with him, although that to speak properly, the lord swears not fealty to his vassal, but he to him; if the law of the twelve tables does detest and hold in execration the protector who defrauds him that is under his tuition; if the civil law permit an enfranchised servant to bring his action against his patron for any grievous usage; if in such cases the same law delivers the slave from the power of his master, although the obligation be natural only and not civil, is it not much more reasonable that the people be loosed from that oath of allegiance which they have taken if the king (who may be not unfitly compared to an attorney sworn to look to his client's cause) first break his oath solemnly taken? And what if all these ceremonies, solemn oaths, nay, sacramental promises had never been taken? Does not nature herself sufficiently teach that kings were on this condition ordained by the people, that they should govern well; judges, that they should distribute justice uprightly; captains in the war, that they should lead their armies against their enemies? If on the contrary they themselves forage and spoil their subjects, and instead of governors become enemies, as they leave indeed the true and essential qualities of a king, so neither ought the people to acknowledge them for lawful princes. But what if a people (you will reply) subdued by force, be compelled by the king to take an oath of servitude? And what if a robber, pirate, or tyrant, I will answer, with whom no bond of human society can be effectual, holding his dagger to your throat, constrain you presently to become bound in a great sum of money? Is it not an unquestionable maxim in law that a promise exacted by violence cannot bind, especially if anything be promised against common reason or the law of nature? Is there anything more repugnant to nature and reason than that a people should manacle and fetter themselves, and to be obliged by promise to the prince with their own hands and weapons to be their own executioners? There is therefore a mutual obligation between the king and the people, which whether it be civil or natural only, whether tacit or expressed in words, it cannot by any means be annihilated or by any law be abrogated, much less by force made void. And this obligation is of such power that the prince who willfully violates it is a tyrant and the people who purposely break it may be justly termed seditious.

Hitherto we have treated of a king. It now rests we do somewhat more fully describe a tyrant. We have showed that he is a king who lawfully governs a kingdom, either derived to him by succession or committed to him by election. It follows therefore that he is reputed a tyrant, which, as opposite to a king, either gains a kingdom by violence or indirect means, or being invested therewith by lawful election or succession governs it not according to law and equity, or neglects those contracts and agreements, to the observation whereof he was strictly obliged at his reception, all which may very well occur in one and the same person. The first is commonly called a tyrant without title, the second a tyrant by practice. Now, it may well so come to pass that he who possesses himself of a kingdom by force, to govern justly, and he on whom it descends by a lawful title, to rule unjustly. But forsomuch as a kingdom is rather a right than an inheritance, and an office than a possession, he seems rather worthy the name of a tyrant who unworthily acquits himself of his charge than he who entered into his place by a wrong door. In the same sense is the pope called an intruder who entered by indirect means into the papacy, and he an abuser who governs ill in it.

Pythagoras says that "a worthy stranger is to be preferred before an unworthy citizen, yea, though he be a kinsman." Let it be lawful also for us to say that a prince who gained his principality by indirect courses, provided he govern according to law and administer justice equally, is much to be preferred before him, who carries himself tyrannously, although he were legally invested into his government with all the ceremonies and rites thereunto appertaining. For seeing that kings were instituted to feed, to judge, to cure the diseases of the people, certainly I had rather that a thief should feed me than a shepherd devour me; I had rather receive justice from a robber than outrage from a judge; I had better be healed by an empiric than poisoned by a doctor in physic. It were much more profitable for me to have my estate carefully managed by an intruding guardian than to have it wasted and dissipated by one legally appointed.

And although it may be that ambition was his first solicitor to enter violently into the government, yet may it perhaps appear he affected it rather to give testimony of his equity and moderation in governing; witness Cyrus, Alexander, and the Romans, who ordinarily accorded to those people they subdued permission to govern themselves according to their own laws, customs, and privileges, yea, sometimes incorporated them into the body of their own state; on the contrary, the tyrant by practice seems to extend the privilege of his legal succession the better to execute violence and extortion, as may be seen in these days, not only by the examples of the Turks and Muscovites, but also in divers Christian princes. Therefore the act of one who at the first was ill is in some reasonable time rectified by justice, whereas the other like an inveterate disease, the older it grows, the worse it affects the patient.

Now, if according to the saying of Saint Augustine, "Those king-doms where justice hath no place are but a rhapsody of freebooters," they are in that both the tyrant without title, and he by practice alike, for that they are both thieves, both robbers, and both unjust possessors, as he certainly is no less an unjust detainer who takes another man's goods against the owner's will than he who employs it ill when it was taken before. But the fault is without comparison much greater of him who possesses an estate to ruin it than of the other who made himself master of it to preserve it. Briefly, the tyrant by practice vainly coloring his unjust extortions with the justice of his title is much more blam-able than the tyrant without title who recompenses the violence of his first intrusion in a continued course of a legal and upright government.

But to proceed, there may be observed some difference amongst tyrants without title, for there are some who ambitiously invade their neighbor's countries to enlarge their own, as Nimrod, Minus, and the Canaanites have done. Although such are termed kings by their own people, yet to those on whose confines they have encroached without any just right or occasion, they will be accounted tyrants. There be others, who having attained to the government of an elective king-dom endeavor by deceitful means, by corruption, by presents, and other bad practices to make it become hereditary. For witness where-of, we need not make search into older times; these are worse than the former forsomuch as secret fraud, as Cicero says, "is ever more odious than open force."

There be also others who are so horribly wicked that they seek to enthrall their own native country like the viperous brood which gnaws through the entrails of their mother, as are those generals of armies created by the people who afterwards by the means of those forces make themselves masters of the stage, as Caesar at Rome under pretense of the dictatorship, and divers princes of Italy.

There be women also who intrude themselves into the government of those kingdoms which the laws only permit to the males, and make themselves queens and regents, as Athaliah did in Judah, Semiramis in Assyria, Agrippina in the Roman empire in the reign of her son Nero, Mammea in the time of Alexander Severus, Semiamira in Heliogabalus's, and certain Bruniehildes in the kingdom of France, who so educated their sons (as the queens of the house of Medicis in these latter times) during their minority that attaining to more maturity their only care was to glut themselves in pleasures and delights, so that the whole management of affairs remained in the hands of their mothers, or of their minions, servants and officers. Those also are tyrants without title who, taking advantage of the sloth, weakness, and dissolute courses of those princes who are otherwise lawfully instituted, and seeking to enwrap them in a sleepy dream of voluptuous idleness (as under the French kings, especially those of the Merovingian line, some of the mayors of the palace have been advanced to that dignity for such egregious services), transferring into their own command all the royal authority and leaving the king only the bare name, all which tyrants are certainly of this condition: that if for the manner of their government they are not blamable. Yet forsomuch as they entered into that jurisdiction by tyrannous intrusion, they may justly be termed tyrants without title.

Concerning tyrants by practice, it is not so easy to describe them as true kings. For reason rules the one, and self-will the other: the first prescribes bounds to his affections, the second confines his desires within no limits. What is the proper rights of kings may be easily declared, but the outrageous insolences of tyrants cannot without much difficulty be expressed. And as a right angle is uniform and like to itself one and the same, so an oblique diversifies itself into various and sundry species. In like manner is justice and equity simple, and may be deciphered in few words, but injustice and injury are divers, and for their sundry accidents not to be so easily defined, but that more will be omitted than expressed. Now, although there be certain rules by which these tyrants may be represented (though not absolutely to the life), yet, notwithstanding, there is not any more certain rule than by conferring and comparing a tyrant's fraudulent slights with a king's virtuous actions.

A tyrant lops off those ears which grow higher than the rest of the corn, especially where virtue makes them most conspicuously eminent; oppresses by calumnies and fraudulent practices the principal officers of the state; gives out reports of intended conspiracies against himself that he might have some colorable pretext to cut them off. Witness Tiberius, Maximinius, and others, who spared not their own kinsmen, cousins, and brothers.

The king, on the contrary, does not only acknowledge his brothers to be as it were consorts unto him in the empire, but also holds in the place of brothers all the principal officers of the kingdom, and is not ashamed to confess that of them (in quality as deputed from the general estates) he holds the crown. The tyrant advances above and in opposition to the ancient and worthy nobility, mean and unworthy persons, to the end that these base fellows, being absolutely his creatures, might applaud and apply themselves to the fulfilling of all his loose and unruly desires. The king maintains every man in his rank, and honors and respects the grandees as the kingdom's friends, desiring their good as well as his own. The tyrant hates and suspects discreet and wise men, and fears no opposition more than virtue as being conscious of his own vicious courses, and esteeming his own security to consist principally in a general corruption of all estates introduces multiplicity of taverns, gaming houses, masks, stage plays, brothel houses, and all other licentious superfluities that might effeminate and bastardize noble spirits, as Cyrus did, to weaken and subdue the Sardiens. The king, on the contrary, allures from all places honest and able men, and encourages them by pensions and honors, and for seminaries of virtue, erects schools and universities in all convenient places.

A tyrant as much as in him lies, prohibits or avoids all public assemblies, fears parliaments, diets and meetings of the general estates, flies the light, affecting (like the bat) to converse only in darkness; yea, he is jealous of the very gesture, countenance, and discourse of his subjects. The king, because he converses always as in the presence of men and angels, glories in the multitude and sufficiency of his counselors, esteeming nothing well done which is ordered without their advice, and is so far from doubting or distasting the public meeting of the general estates as he honors and respects those assemblies with much favor and affection.

A tyrant nourishes and feeds factions and dissensions amongst his subjects, ruins one by the help of another that he may the easier vanquish the remainder, advantaging himself by this division like those dishonest surgeons who lengthen out their cures. Briefly, after the manner of that abominable Vitellius, he is not ashamed to say that the carcass of a dead enemy, especially a subject's, yields a good savor. On the contrary, a good king endeavors always to keep peace amongst his subjects, as a father amongst his children, choke the seeds of troubles, and quickly heals the scar; the execution, even of justice upon rebels, drawing tears from his compassionate eyes, yea, those whom a good king maintains and defends against a foreign enemy, a tyrant (the enemy of nature) compels them to turn the points of their swords into their own proper entrails. A tyrant fills his garrisons with strange soldiers, builds citadels against his subjects, disarms the people, throws down their forts, makes himself formidable with guards of strangers, or men only fit for pillage and spoil, gives pensions out of the public treasury to spies and calumniating informers dispersed through all cities and provinces. Contrariwise, a king reposes more his safety in the love of his subjects than in the strength of his fortresses against his enemies, taking no care to enroll soldiers, but accounts every subject as a man-at-arms to guard him, and builds forts to restrain the eruptions of foreign enemies, and not to constrain his subjects to obedience, in whose fidelity he puts his greatest confidence. Therefore it is that tyrants, although they have such numberless guards about them to drive off throngs of people from approaching them, yet cannot all those numbers secure them from doubts, jealousies, and distrusts, which continually afflict and terrify their timorous consciences, yea, in the midst of their greatest strength, the tyrannizer of tyrants, fear, makes prize of their souls, and there triumphs in their affliction.

A good king, in the greatest concourse of people, is freest from doubts or fears, nor troubled with solicitous distrusts in his solitary retirements; all places are equally secure unto him, his own conscience being his best guard. If a tyrant wants civil broils to exercise his cruel disposition in, he makes wars abroad, and erects idle and needless trophies to continually employ his tributaries, that they might not have leisure to think on other things, as Pharaoh did the Jews, and Policrates the Samians; therefore he always prepares for or threatens war, or at least seems so to do, and so still rather draws mischief on than puts it further off. A king never makes war, but compelled unto it, and for the preservation of the public, he never desires to purchase advantage by treason; he never enters into any war that exposes the commonwealth to more danger than it affords probable hope of commodity.

A tyrant leaves no design unattempted by which he may fleece his subjects of their substance, and turn it to his proper benefit, that being continually troubled in gaining means to live, they may have no leisure, no hope how to regain their liberty. On the contrary, the king knows that every good subject's purse will be ready to supply the commonwealth occasion, and therefore believes he is possessed of no small treasure, whilst through his good government his subjects flow in all abundance.

A tyrant extorts unjustly from many to cast prodigally upon two or three minions, and those unworthy; he imposes on all and exacts from all to furnish their superfluous and riotous expenses; he builds his own and followers' fortunes on the ruins of the public; he draws out the people's blood by the veins of their means, and gives it presently to carouse to his court-leeches. But a king cuts off from his ordinary expenses to ease the people's necessities, neglects his private state, and furnishes with all magnificence the public occasions; briefly is prodigal of his own blood, to defend and maintain the people committed to his care.

If a tyrant, as heretofore Tiberius, Nero, Commodus and others, did suffer his subjects to have some breathing time from unreasonable exactions, and like sponges to gather some moisture, it is but to squeeze them out afterwards to his own use; on the contrary, if a king do sometimes open a vein, and draw some blood, it is for the people's good, and not to be expended at his own pleasure in any dissolute courses.

And therefore, as the Holy Scripture compares the one to a shepherd, so does it also resemble the other to a roaring lion, to whom notwithstanding the fox is oftentimes coupled. For a tyrant, as says Cicero, "is culpable in effect of the greatest injustice that may be imagined, and yet he carries it so cunningly that when he most deceives it is then that he makes greatest appearance to deal sincerely." And therefore does he artificially counterfeit religion and devotion, wherein saith Aristotle, "He expresses one of the most absolute subtleties that tyrants can possibly practice: he does so compose his countenance to piety, by that means to terrify the people from conspiring against him, who they may well imagine to be especially favored of God, expressing in all appearance so reverently to serve Him." He feigns also to be exceedingly affected to the public good; not so much for the love of it as for fear of his own safety. Furthermore, he desires much to be esteemed just and loyal in some affairs, purposely to deceive and betray more easily in matters of greater consequence, much like those thieves who maintain themselves by thefts and robberies, yet cannot long subsist in their trade without exercising some parcel of justice in their proceedings. He also counterfeits the merciful, but it is in pardoning of such malefactors, in punishing whereof he might more truly gain the reputation of a pitiful prince. To speak in a word: that which the true king is, the tyrant would seem to be, and knowing that men are wonderfully attracted with and enamored of virtue, he endeavors with much subtlety to make his vices appear yet masked with some shadow of virtue, but let him counterfeit never so cunningly, still the fox will be known by his tail, and although he fawn and flatter like a spaniel, yet his snarling and grinning will ever betray his currish kind.

Furthermore, as a well-ordered monarchy partakes of the principal commodities of all other governments, so, on the contrary, where tyranny prevails, there all the discommodities of confusion are frequent. A monarchy has in this conformity with an aristocracy: that the most able and discreet are called to consultations. Tyranny and oligarchy accord in this: that their councils are composed of the worst and most corrupted. And as in the council royal, there may in a sort seem many kings to have interests in the government, so in the other, on the contrary, a multitude of tyrants always domineers.

The monarchy borrows of the popular government the assemblies of the estates, whither are sent for deputies the most sufficient of cities and provinces, to deliberate on and determine matters of state. The tyranny takes this of the ochlocracy: that if she be not able to hinder the convocation of the estates, yet will she endeavor by factious subtleties and pernicious practices that the greatest enemies of order and reformation of the state be sent to those assemblies, the which we have known practiced in our times. In this manner assumes the tyrant the countenance of a king, and tyranny the semblance of a kingdom, and the continuance succeeds commonly according to the dexterity wherewith it is managed, yet as Aristotle says, "We shall hardly read of any tyranny that has outlasted a hundred years." Briefly, the king principally regards the public utility, and a tyrant's chiefest care is for his private commodity.

But seeing the condition of men is such that a king is with much difficulty to be found that in all his actions he only agrees at the public good, and yet cannot long subsist without expression of some special care thereof, we will conclude that where the commonwealth's advantage is most preferred, there is both a lawful king and kingdom, and where particular designs and private ends prevail against the public profit, there questionless is a tyrant and tyranny.

Thus much concerning tyrants by practice, in the examining whereof we have not altogether fixed our discourse on the loose disorders of their wicked and licentious lives, which some say is the character of a bad man, but not always of a bad prince. If therefore the reader be not satisfied with this description, besides the more exact representations of tyrants which he shall find in histories, he may in these our days behold an absolute model of many living and breathing tyrants, whereof Aristotle in his time did much complain. Now at the last we are come as it were by degrees to the chief and principal point of the question. We have seen how that kings have been chosen by God, either with relation to their families or their persons only, and after installed by the people. In like manner what is the duty of the king, and of the officers of the kingdom, how far the authority, power, and duty both of the one and the other extends, and what and how sacred are the covenants and contracts which are made at the inauguration of kings, and what conditions are intermixed, both tacit and expressed; finally, who is a tyrant without title, and who by practice, seeing it is a thing unquestionable that we are bound to obey a lawful king, which both to God and people carries himself according to those covenants whereunto he stands obliged, as it were to God Himself, seeing in a sort he represents His divine Majesty? It now follows that we treat, how, and by whom a tyrant may be lawfully resisted, and who are the persons who ought to be chiefly actors therein, and what course is to be held that the action may be managed according to right and reason. We must first speak of him who is commonly called a tyrant without title. Let us suppose then that some Ninus, having neither received outrage nor offense, invades a people over whom he has no color of pretension; that Caesar seeks to oppress his country, and the Roman commonwealth; that Popiclus endeavors by murders and treasons to make the elective kingdom of Polonia to become hereditary to him and his posterity; or some Bruniehilde draws to herself and her Protadius the absolute government of France; or Ebronius, taking advantage of Theodoric's weakness and idleness, gains the entire administration of the state and oppresses the people, what shall be our lawful refuge herein?

First, the law of nature teaches and commands us to maintain and defend our lives and liberties, without which life is scant worth the enjoying, against all injury and violence. Nature has imprinted this by instinct in dogs against wolves, in bulls against lions, betwixt pigeons and sparrow-hawks, betwixt pullen and kites, and yet much more in man against man himself, if man become a beast: and therefore he who questions the lawfulness of defending oneself, does, as much as in him lies, question the law of nature. To this must be added the law of nations, which distinguishes possessions and dominions, fixes limits, and makes out confines, which every man is bound to defend against all invaders. And therefore it is no less lawful to resist Alexander the Great, if without any right or being justly provoked, he invades a country with a mighty navy, as well as Diomedes the pirate who scours the seas in a small vessel. For in this case Alexander's right is no more than Diomedes' but only he has more power to do wrong, and not so easily to be compelled to reason as the other. Briefly, one may as well oppose Alexander in pillaging a country as a thief in purloining a cloak; as well him when he seeks to batter down the walls of a city as a robber who offers to break into a private house.

There is, besides this, the civil law, or municipal laws of several countries which governs the societies of men, by certain rules, some in one manner, some in another; some submit themselves to the government of one man, some to more; others are ruled by a whole commonalty, some absolutely exclude women from the royal throne, others admit them; these here choose their king descended of such a family, those there make election of whom they please, besides other customs practiced amongst several nations. If therefore any offer either by fraud or force to violate this law, we are all bound to resist him because he wrongs that society to which we owe all that we have, and would ruin our country, to the preservation whereof all men by nature by law and by solemn oath are strictly obliged. Insomuch that fear or negligence, or bad purposes make us omit this duty, we may justly be accounted breakers of the laws, betrayers of our country, and condemners of religion. Now as the laws of nature, of nations, and the Civil commands us to take arms against such tyrants, so is there not any manner of reason that should persuade us to the contrary; neither is there any oath, covenant, or obligation, public or private, of power justly to restrain us; therefore the meanest private man may resist and lawfully oppose such an intruding tyrant. The Lex Julia, which condemns to death those who raise rebellion against their country or prince, has here no place; for he is no prince who without any lawful title invades the commonwealth or confines of another; nor he a rebel who by arms defends his country, but rather to this had relation the oath which all the youth of Athens were accustomed to take in the temple of Aglaura: "I will fight for religion, for the laws, for the altars, and for our possessions, either alone or with others, and will do the utmost of my endeavor to leave to posterity our country, at the least in as good estate as I found it." To as little purpose can the laws made against seditious persons be alleged here, for he is seditious who undertakes to defend the people in opposition of order and public discipline; but he is no raiser but a suppressor of sedition who restrains within the limits of reason the subverter of his country's welfare and public discipline.

On the contrary, to this has proper relation the law of tyrannicide, which honors the living with great and memorable recompenses, and the dead with worthy epitaphs and glorious statues, that have been their country's liberators from tyrants; as Harmodius and Aristogiton at Athens, Brutus and Cassius in Rome, and Aratus of Sycione. To these by a public decree were erected statues because they delivered their countries from the tyrannies of Pisistratus, of Caesar, and of Nicocles, the which was of such respect amongst the ancients, that Xerxes having made himself master of the city of Athens, caused to be transported into Persia the statues of Harmodius and Aristogiton; afterwards Seleucus caused them to be returned into their former place, and as in their passage they came by Rhodes, those famous citizens entertained them with public and stupendous solemnities, and during their abode there, they placed them in the choicest sacresties of their gods. But the law made against forsakers and traitors takes absolutely hold on those who are negligent and careless to deliver their country oppressed with tyranny, and condemns them to the same punishment as those cowardly soldiers who, when they should fight, either counterfeit sickness or cast off their arms and run away. Everyone, therefore, both in general and particular, ought to yield their best assistance unto this: as in a public fire, to bring both hooks, and buckets, and water; we must not ceremoniously expect that the captain of the watch be first called, nor till the governor of the town be come into the streets; but let every man draw water and climb to the house-top; it is necessary for all men that the fire be quenched. For if whilst the Gauls with much silence and vigilance seek to scale and surprise the capital the soldiers be drowsy with their former pains, the watch buried in sleep, the dogs fail to bark, then must the geese play the sentinels and with their cackling noise, give an alarm. And the soldiers and watch shall be degraded, yea, and put to death. The geese for perpetual remembrance of this deliverance shall be always fed in the capital and much esteemed.

This, of which we have spoken, is to be understood of a tyranny not yet firmly rooted: to wit, whilst a tyrant conspires, machinates, and lays his plots and practices. But if he be once so possessed of the state, and the people, being subdued, promise and swear obedience; the commonwealth being oppressed, resign their authority into their hands; and the kingdom in some formal manner consent to the changing of their laws, forsomuch certainty as then he has gained a title which before he wanted and seems to be as well a legal as actual possessor thereof, although this yoke were laid on the people's neck by compulsion, yet must they quietly and peaceably rest in the will of the Almighty, who at His pleasure transfers kingdoms from one nation to another; otherwise there should be no kingdom whose jurisdiction might not be disputed. And it may well chance that he who before was a tyrant without title, having obtained the title of a king, may free himself from any tyrannous imputation by governing those under him with equity and moderation. Therefore then, as the people of Judah under the authority of King Hezekiah did lawfully resist the invasion of Sennacherib the Assyrian, so on the contrary was Zedekiah and all his subjects worthily punished, because that without any just occasion, after they had done homage and sworn fealty to Nebuchadnezzar, they rose in rebellion against him. For after promise of performance, it is too late to repent. And as in battles everyone ought to give testimony of his valor, but being taken prisoner must faithfully observe covenants, so it is requisite that the people maintain their rights by all possible means; but if it chance that they be brought into the subjection of another's will, they must then patiently support the dominion of the victor. So did Pompey, Cato, and Cicero and others perform the parts of good patriots then when they took arms against Caesar, seeking to alter the government of the state; neither can those be justly excused whose base fear hindered the happy success of Pompey and his partakers' noble designs. Augustus himself is said to have reproved one who railed on Cato, affirming that he carried himself worthily and exceedingly affected to the greatness of his country in courageously opposing the alteration which his contraries sought to introduce in the government of the state, seeing all innovations of that nature are ever authors of much trouble and confusion.

Furthermore, no man can justly reprehend Brutus, Cassius, and the rest who killed Caesar before his tyrannical authority had taken any firm rooting. And so there were statues of brass erected in honor of them by public decree at Athens, and placed by those of Harmodius and Aristogiton; then after the dispatching of Caesar they retired from Rome to avoid Mark Antonie and Augustus their revenge. But Cinna was certainly guilty of sedition, who after a legal transferring of the people's power into the hands of Augustus is said to have conspired against him. Likewise, when the Pepins sought to take the crown of France from the Merovingians; as also when those of the line of Capet endeavored to supplant the Pepins, any might lawfully resist them without incurring the crime of sedition. But when by public counsel and the authority of the estates, the kingdom was transferred from one family to another, it was then unlawful to oppose it. The same may be said if a woman possess herself of the kingdom, which the Salic law absolutely prohibits, or if one seek to make a kingdom merely elective hereditary to his offspring, while those laws stand in force, and are unrepealed by the authority of the general estates, who represent the body of the people. Neither is it necessary in this respect to have regard whether faction is the greater, more powerful, or more illustrious. Always those are the greater number who are led by passion than those who are ruled by reason, and therefore tyranny has more servants than the commonwealth. But Rome is there, according to the saying of Pompey, where the senate is, and the senate is where there is obedience to the laws, love of liberty, and studious carefulness for the country's preservation. And therefore, though Brennus may seem to be master of Rome, yet notwithstanding is Rome at Veii with Camillus, who prepares to deliver Rome from bondage. It behooves therefore all true Romans to repair to Camillus and assist his enterprise with the utmost of their power and endeavors. Although Themistocles, and all his able and worthiest companions leave Athens and put to sea with a navy of two hundred galleys, notwithstanding it cannot be said that any of these men are banished Athens, but rather as Themistocles answered, "These two hundred galleys are more useful for us than the greatest city of all Greece; for that they are armed and prepared for the defense of those who endeavor to maintain and uphold the public state."

But to come to other examples, it follows not that the church of God must needs be always in that place where the ark of the covenant is; for the Philistines may carry the ark into the temples of their idols. It is no good argument that because we see the Roman eagles waving in ensigns and hear their legions named that therefore presently we conclude that the army of the Roman commonwealth is there present; for there is only and properly the power of the state where they are assembled to maintain the liberty of the country against the ravenous oppression of tyrants, to enfranchise the people from servitude, and to suppress the impudence of insulting flatterers who abuse the prince's weakness by oppressing his subjects for the advantage of their own fortunes, and contain ambitious minds from enlarging their desires beyond the limits of equity and moderation. Thus much concerning tyrants without title.

But for tyrants by practice, whether they at first gained their authority by the sword, or were legally invested there with by a general consent, it behooves us to examine this point with much wary circumspection. In the first place we must remember that all princes are born men, and therefore reason and passion are as hardly to be separated in them as the soul is from the body whilst the man lives. We must not then expect princes absolute in perfection, but rather repute ourselves happy if those who govern us be indifferently good. And therefore although the prince observe not exact mediocrity in state affairs, if sometimes passion overrule his reason, if some careless omission make him neglect the public utility, or if he do not always carefully execute justice with equality, or repulse not with ready valor an invading enemy, he must not therefore be presently declared a tyrant. And certainly, seeing he rules not as a god over men, nor as men over beasts, but is a man composed of the same matter, and of the same nature with the rest, as we would questionless judge that prince unreasonably insolent who should insult over and abuse his subjects as if they were brute beasts, so those people are doubtless as much void of reason who imagine a prince should be complete in perfection or expect divine abilities in a nature so frail and subject to imperfections. But if a prince purposely ruin the commonwealth if he presumptuously pervert and resist legal proceedings or lawful rights; if he make no reckoning of faith, covenants, justice nor piety; if he prosecute his subjects as enemies; briefly, if he express all or the chiefest of those wicked practices we have formerly spoken of, then we may certainly declare him a tyrant who is as much an enemy both to God and men. We do not therefore speak of a prince less good, but of one absolutely bad; not of one less wise, but of one malicious and treacherous; not of one less able judiciously to discuss legal differences, but of one perversely bent to pervert justice and equity; not of an unwarlike one, but of one furiously disposed to ruin the people and ransack the state.

For the wisdom of a senate, the integrity of a judge, the valor of a captain may peradventure enable a weak prince to govern well. But a tyrant could be content that all the nobility, the counselors of state, the commanders for the wars had but one head that he might take it off at one blow, those being the proper objects of his distrust and fear, and by consequence the principal subjects on whom he desires to execute his malice and cruelty. A foolish prince, although (to speak according to right and equity) he ought to be deposed, yet may he perhaps in some sort be borne withal. But a tyrant the more he is tolerated, the more he becomes intolerable.

Furthermore, as the prince's pleasure is not always law, so many times it is not expedient that the people do all that which may lawfully be done; for it may oftentimes chance that the medicine proves more dangerous than the disease. Therefore it becomes wise men to try all ways before they come to blows, to use all other remedies before they suffer the sword to decide the controversy. If then those who represent the body of the people foresee any innovation or machination against the state, or that it be already embarked into a course of perdition, their duty is first to admonish the prince, and not to attend, that the disease by accession of time and accidents becomes unrecoverable. For tyranny may be properly resembled unto a fever hectic, the which at the first is easy to be cured, but with much difficulty to be known; but after it is sufficiently known, it becomes incurable. Therefore small beginnings are to be carefully observed, and by those whom it concerns diligently prevented.

If the prince therefore persist in his violent courses, and condemn frequent admonitions, addressing his designs only to that end that he may oppress at his pleasure and effect his own desires without fear or restraint; he then doubtless makes himself liable to that detested crime of tyranny, and whatsoever either the law or lawful authority permits against a tyrant may be lawfully practiced against him. Tyranny is not only a will, but the chief, and as it were the complement and abstract of vices. A tyrant subverts the state, pillages the people, lays stratagems to entrap their lives, breaks promise with all, scoffs at the sacred obligations of a solemn oath, and therefore is he so much more vile than the vilest of usual malefactors. By how much offenses committed against a generality are worthy of greater punishment than those which concern only particular and private persons. If thieves and those who commit sacrilege be declared infamous, nay, if they justly suffer corporal punishment by death, can we invent any that may be worthily equivalent for so outrageous a crime?

Furthermore, we have already proved that all kings receive their royal authority from the people; that the whole people considered in one body is above and greater than the king; and that the king and emperor are only the prime and supreme governors and ministers of the kingdom and empire, but the people the absolute lord and owner thereof. It therefore necessarily follows that a tyrant is in the same manner guilty of rebellion against the majesty of the people, as the lord of a fee who feloniously transgresses the conditions of his investitures and is liable to the same punishment, yea, and certainly deserves much more greater than the equity of those laws inflicts on the delinquents. Therefore as Bartolus says, "He may either be deposed by those who are lords in sovereignty over him, or else justly punished according to the Lex Julia, which condemns those who offer violence to the public." The body of the people must needs be the sovereign of those who represent it, which in some places are the electors, palatines, peers; in others, the assembly of the general estates. And, if the tyranny have gotten such sure footing as there is no other means but force to remove him, then it is lawful for them to call the people to arms, to enroll and raise forces, and to employ the utmost of their power, and use against him all advantages and stratagems of war as against the enemy of the commonwealth and the disturber of the public peace. Briefly, the same sentence may be justly pronounced against him, as was against Manlius Capitolinus at Rome. "you wast to me, Manlius, when you didst tumble down the Gauls that scaled the capital, but since you are now become an enemy, like one of them, you shall be precipitated down from the same place from whence you formerly tumbled those enemies." The officers of the kingdom cannot for this be rightly accused of sedition; for in a sedition there must necessarily concur but two parts or sides, the which peremptorily contest together, so that it is necessary that the one be in the right, and the other in the wrong. That part undoubtedly has the right on their side which defends the laws and strives to advance the public profit of the kingdom. And those on the contrary are questionless in the wrong who break the laws and protect those who violate justice and oppress the commonwealth. Those are certainly in the right way, as said Bartolus, "who endeavor to suppress tyrannical government, and those in the wrong who oppose lawful authority." And that must ever be accounted just which is intended only for the public benefit, and that unjust which aims chiefly at private commodity. Wherefore Thomas Aquinas says that "a tyrannical rule, having no proper address for the public welfare, but only to satisfy a private will, with increase of particular profit to the ruler, cannot in any reasonable construction be accounted lawful, and therefore the disturbance of such a government cannot be esteemed seditious, much less traitorous"; for offense has proper relation only to a lawful prince, who indeed is an inanimated or speaking law; therefore, seeing that he who employs the utmost of his means and power to annihilate the laws and quell their virtue and vigor, can nowise be justly entitled therewith. So neither, likewise, can those who oppose and take arms against him be branded with so notorious a crime. Also this offense is committed against the commonwealth, but forsomuch as the commonwealth is there only where the laws are in force, and not where a tyrant devours the state at his own pleasure and liking, he certainly is quit of that crime which ruins the majesty of the public state, and those questionless are worthily protectors and preservers of the commonwealth, who confident in the lawfulness of their authority and summoned thereunto by their duty do courageously resist the unjust proceedings of the tyrant.

And in this their action, we must not esteem them as private men and subjects, but as the representative body of the people, yea, and as the sovereignty itself, which demands of his minister an account of his administration. Neither can we in any good reason account the

officers of the kingdom disloyal, who in this manner acquit themselves of their charge.

There is ever and in all places a mutual and reciprocal obligation
between the people and the prince; the one promises to be a good and
wise prince, the other to obey faithfully, provided he govern justly. The
people therefore are obliged to the prince under condition, the prince
to the people simply and purely. Therefore, if the prince fail in his
promise, the people are exempt from obedience, the contract is made
void, the right of obligation of no force. Then the king if he govern
unjustly is perjured, and the people likewise forsworn if they obey not
his lawful commands. But that people are truly acquit from all per-
fidiousness who publicly renounce the unjust dominion of a tyrant,
or he, striving unjustly by strong hand to continue the possession, do
constantly endeavor to expulse him by force of arms.

It is therefore permitted the officers of a kingdom, either all or
some good number of them, to suppress a tyrant, and it is not only
lawful for them to do it, but their duty expressly requires it, and if they
do it not, they can by no excuse color their baseness. For the electors,
palatines, peers, and other officers of state must not think they were
established only to make pompous paradoes and shows, when they
are at the coronation of the king, habited in their robes of state, as if
there were some masque or interlude to be represented; or as if they
were that day to act the parts of Roland, Oliver, or Renaldo, and such
other personages on a stage, or to counterfeit and revive the memory
of the knights of the round table; and after the dismissing of that
day's assembly, to suppose they have sufficiently acquitted themselves
of their duty, until a recess of the like solemnity. Those solemn rites
and ceremonies were not instituted for vain ostentation, nor to pass,
as in a dumb show, to please the spectators, nor in children's sports,
as it is with Horace, to create a king in jest, but those grandees must
know that as well for office and duty as for honor they are called to
the performance of those rites, and that in them the commonwealth

is committed and recommended to the king, as to her supreme and principal tutor and protector, and to them as co-adjutors and assistants to him, and therefore, as the tutors or guardians (yea, even those who are appointed by way of honor) are chosen to have care of and observe the actions and importments of him who holds the principal rank in the tutorship, and to look how he carries himself in the administration of the goods of his pupil. So likewise are the former ordained to have an eye to the courses of the king; for with an equivalent authority, as the others for the pupil, so are they to hinder and prevent the damage and detriment of the people, the king being properly reputed as the prime guardian and they his co-adjutors.

In like manner, as the faults of the principal tutor who manages the affairs are justly imputed to the co-adjoints in the tutorship, if when they ought and might they did not discover his errors and cause him to be despoiled, especially failing in the main points of his charge, to wit, in not communicating unto them the affairs of his administration, in dealing unfaithfully in his place, in doing anything to the dishonor or detriment of his pupil, in embezzling of his goods or estate, or if he be an enemy to his pupil; briefly, if either in regard of the worthlessness of his person or weakness of his judgment, he be unable well to discharge so weighty a charge, so also are the peers and principal officers of the kingdom accountable for the government thereof, and must both prevent, and if occasion require, suppress the tyranny of the prince, as also supply with their care and diligence his inability and weakness.

Finally, if a tutor omitting or neglecting to do all that for his pupil which a discreet father of a family would and might conveniently perform, cannot well be excused, and the better acquitting himself of his charge, has others as concealers and associates joined with him to oversee his actions, with much more reason may and ought the officers of the crown to restrain the violent irruptions of that prince who, instead of a father, becomes an enemy to his people, seeing, to speak properly, they are as well accountable for his actions wherein the public has interests as for their own.

Those officers must also remember that the king holds truly the first place in the administration of the state, but they the second, and so following according to their ranks; not that they should follow his courses if he transgress the laws of equity and justice; not that if he oppress the commonwealth they should connive to his wickedness. For the commonwealth was as well committed to their care as to his, so that it is not sufficient for them to discharge their own duty in particular, but it behooves them also to contain the prince within the limits of reason; briefly, they have both jointly and severally promised with solemn oaths to advance and procure the profit of a commonwealth, although he forswore himself; yet may not they imagine that they are quit of their promise, no more than the bishops and patriarchs if they suffer an heretical pope to ruin the church, yea, they should esteem themselves so much the more obliged to the observing their oath by how much they find him willfully disposed to rush on in his perfidious courses. But if there be collusion betwixt him and them, they are prevaricators; if they dissemble, they may justly be called forsakers and traitors; if they deliver not the commonwealth from tyranny, they may be truly ranked in the number of tyrants, as on the contrary they are protectors, tutors, and in a sort kings, if they keep and maintain the state safe and entire, which is also recommended to their care and custody.

Although these things are sufficiently certain of themselves, yet may they be in some sort confirmed by examples. The kings of Canaan who pressed the people of Israel with a hard both corporal and spiritual servitude (prohibiting them all meetings and use of arms) were certainly tyrants by practice, although they had some pretext of title. For Eglon and Jabin had peaceably reigned almost the space of twenty years. God stirred up extraordinarily Ehud, who by a politic stratagem killed Eglon, and Deborah who overthrew the army of

Jabin, and by his service delivered the people from the servitude of tyrants; not that it was unlawful for the ordinary magistrates, the princes of the tribes, and such other officers to have performed it, for Deborah does reprove the sluggish idleness of some, and flatly detests the disloyalty of others, because they failed to perform their duty herein. But it pleased God, taking commiseration of the distress of his people, in this manner to supply the defects of the ordinary magistrates.

Rehoboam, the son of Solomon, refused to disburden the people of some unnecessary imposts and burdens, and being petitioned by the people in the general assembly of the states, he grew insolent, and relying on the counsel of his minions, arrogantly threatens to lay heavier burdens on them hereafter. No man can doubt but that according to the tenure of the contract first passed between the king and the people, the prime and principal officers of the kingdom had authority to repress such insolence. They were only blamable in this: that they did that by faction and division which should more properly have been done in the general assembly of the states; in like manner, in that they transferred the scepter from Judah (which was by God only confined to that tribe) into another lineage, and also (as it chances in other affairs) for that they did ill and disorderly manage a just and lawful cause. Profane histories are full of such examples in other kingdoms.

Brutus, general of the soldiers, and Lucretius, governor of the city of Rome, assembled the people against Tarquinius Superbus, and by their authority thrust him from the royal throne; nay, which is more, his goods were confiscated, whereby it appears that if Tarquinius had been apprehended, undoubtedly he should have been according to the public laws corporally punished.

The true causes why Tarquinius was deposed were because he altered the custom whereby the king was obliged to advise with the senate on all weighty affairs; that he made war and peace according to his own fancy; that he treated confederacies without demanding counsel and consent from the people or senate; that he violated the laws whereof he was made guardian; briefly that he made no reckoning to observe the contracts agreed between the former kings and the nobility and people of Rome. For the Roman emperors, I am sure you remember the sentence pronounced by the senate against Nero, wherein he was judged an enemy to the commonwealth, and his body condemned to be ignominiously cast on the dung hill, and that other pronounced against Vitellius, which adjudged him to be shamefully dismembered; and in that miserable estate dragged through the city, and at last put to death; another against Maximinius, who was despoiled of the empire, and Maximus and Albinus established in his place by the senate. There might also be added many others drawn from unquestionable historians.

The Emperor Trajan held not himself exempt from laws, neither desired he to be spared if he became a tyrant; for in delivering the sword unto the great provost of the empire, he says unto him: "If I command as I should, use this sword for me, but if I do otherwise, unsheathe it against me." In like manner the French by the authority of the states, solicited thereunto by the officers of the kingdom, deposed Childerick the First, Sigisbert, Theodoric, and Childerick the Third for their tyrannies, and chose others of another family to sit on the royal throne. Yea, they deposed some because of their idleness and want of judgment who exposed the state in prey to panders, courtesans, flatterers, and such other unworthy mushrooms of the court who governed all things at their pleasure, taking from such rash phaetons the bridle of government, lest the whole body of the state and people should be consumed through their unadvised folly.

Amongst others, Theodoret was degraded because of Ebroinus, Dagobert for Plectude and Thibaud his pander, with some others, the estates esteeming the command of an effeminate prince as insupportable as that of a woman, and as unwillingly supporting the yoke of tyrannous ministers managing affairs in the name of a loose and unworthy prince as the burden of a tyrant alone; to be brief, no more suffering themselves to be governed by one possessed by a devil than they would by the devil himself. It is not very long since the estates compelled Lewis the Eleventh (a prince as subtle and it may be as willful as any) to receive thirty-six overseers, by whose advice he was bound to govern the affairs of state. The descendants from Charlemagne substituted in the place of the Merovingians for the government of the kingdom, or those of Capet, supplanting the Charlemagnes by order of the estates and reigning at this day, have no other nor better right to the crown than what we have formerly described; and it has ever been according to law permitted the whole body of the people, represented by the council of the kingdom, which are commonly called the assembly of the states, to depose and establish princes according to the necessities of the commonwealth. According to the same rule we read that Adolph was removed from the Empire of Germany in A.D. 1296, because for covetousness without any just occasion he invaded the kingdom of France in favor of the English, and Wenceslaus was also deposed in the year of our Lord 1400. Yet were not these princes exceedingly bad ones, but of the number of those who are accounted less ill. Isabella, the wife of Edward the Second, king of England, assembled the Parliament against her husband, who was there deposed, both because he tyrannized in general over his subjects, and also for cutting off the heads of many noblemen without any just or legal proceeding. It is not long since Christian lost the crown of Denmark, Henry that of Sweden, Mary Stuart that of Scotland for the same or near resembling occasions. And the most worthy histories relate divers alterations and changes which have happened in like manner in the kingdoms of Polonia, Hungary, Spain, Portugal, Bohemia, and others.

But what shall we say of the pope himself? It is generally held that the cardinals, because they do elect him, or if they fail in their

duty, the patriarchs who are next in rank to them, may upon certain
occasions maugre the pope, call a council, yea, and in it judge him, as
when by some notorious offence he scandalizes the universal church,
if he be incorrigible, if reformation be as necessary in the head as
the members, if contrary to his oath he refuse to call a general council. And we read for certain that divers popes have been deposed by
general councils. But if they obstinately abuse their authority, there
must, says Baldus, first be used verbal admonitions; secondly, herbal
medicaments or remedies; thirdly, stones or compulsion; for where
virtue and fair means have not power to persuade, there force and
terror must be put in use to compel. Now if according to the opinions
of most of the learned, by decrees of councils, and by custom in like
occasions, it plainly appears that the council may depose the pope
who notwithstanding vaunts himself to be the king of kings, and as
much in dignity above the emperor as the sun is above the moon,
assuming to himself power to depose kings and emperors when he
pleases, who will make any doubt or question that the general assembly of the estates of any kingdom, who are the representative body
thereof, may not only degrade and disthronize a tyrant, but also even
disauthorize and depose a king, whose weakness or folly is hurtful or
pernicious to the state?

But let us suppose that in this our ship of state the pilot is drunk,
the most of his associates are asleep, or after large and unreasonable
tippling together, they regard their eminent danger in approaching
a rock with idle and negligent jollity, the ship in the mean season
instead of following her right course, that might serve for the best
advantage of the owners' profit is ready rather to split herself. What
should then a master's mate or some other under officer do who is
vigilant and careful to perform his duty? Shall it be thought sufficient
for him to pinch or punch those who are asleep without daring in the
meantime to put his helping hand to preserve the vessel which runs
on a course to destruction, lest he should be thought to intermeddle

with that which he has no authority nor warrant to do? What mad discretion, nay, rather notorious impiety were this? Seeing then that tyranny, as Plato says, "is a drunken frenzy or frantic drunkenness," if the prince endeavor to ruin the commonwealth, and the principal officers concur with him in his bad purposes, or at the least are lulled in a dull and drowsy dream of security, and the people (being indeed the true and absolute owner and lord of the state) be, through the pernicious negligence and fraudulent connivance of those officers, brought to the very brim of danger and destruction, and that there be notwithstanding amongst those unworthy ministers of state someone who does studiously observe the deceitful and dangerous encroachments of tyranny, and from his soul detests it, what opposition do we suppose best befits such a one to make against it? Shall he consent himself to admonish his associates of their duty, who to their utmost ability endeavor the contrary? Besides, that such an advertisement is commonly accompanied with too much danger, and the condition of the times considered, the very soliciting of reformation will be held as a capital crime, so that in so doing he may be not unfitly resembled to one who, being in the midst of a desert, environed with thieves, should neglect all means of defense, and after he had cast away his arms, in an eloquent and learned discourse commend justice, and extol the worth and dignity of the laws. This would be truly according to the proverb, "To run mad with reason."

What then? Shall he be dull and deaf to the groans and cries of the people? Shall he stand still and be silent when he sees the thieves enter? Shall he only hold his hands in his bosom and with a demure countenance idly bewail the miserable condition of the times? If the laws worthily condemn a soldier who for fear of the enemies counterfeits sickness, because in so doing he expresses both disloyalty and treachery, what punishment can we invent sufficient for him who either maliciously or basely betrays those whose protection and defense he has absolutely under taken and sworn? Nay, rather than let such a one cheerfully call one and command the mariners to the performance of their duty, let him carefully and constantly take order that the commonwealth be not endamaged, and if need so require, even in despite of the king, preserve the kingdom, without which the kingly title were idle and frivolous, and if by no other means it can be affected, let him take the king and bind him hand and foot, so he may be more conveniently cured of his frenzy and madness.

For as we have already said, all the administration of the kingdom is not by the people absolutely resigned into the hands of the king, as neither the bishopric nor care of the universal church is totally committed to the pope, but also to the care and custody of all the principal officers of the kingdom. Now, for the preserving of peace and concord amongst those who govern, and for the preventing of jealousies, factions, and distrusts amongst men of equal rank and dignity, the king was created prime and principal superintendent in the government of the commonwealth. The king swears that his most special care shall be for the welfare of the kingdom, and the officers of the crown take all the same oath. If then the king or divers of them falsifying their faith ruin the commonwealth or abandon her in her greatest necessity, must the rest also fashion themselves to their base courses and quit all care of the state's safety, as if the bad example of their companions absolved them from their oath of fidelity? Nay, rather on the contrary, in seeing them neglect their promise, they shall best advantage the commonwealth in carefully observing theirs, chiefly because for this reason they were instituted, as in the steads of ephori, or public controllers, and since everything gains the better estimation of just and right in that it is mainly and principally addressed to that end for which it was first ordained.

Furthermore, if divers have jointly vowed one and the same thing, is the obligation of the one annihilated by the perjury of the other? If many become bound for one and the same sum, can the bankrupting of one of the obligees quit the rest of their engagement? If divers tutors administer ill the goods of their pupil, and that there be one amongst them who makes conscience of his actions, can the bad dealing of his companions acquit him? Nay rather on the contrary, he cannot free himself from the infamy of perjury if to the utmost of his power he do not truly discharge his trust and perform his promise; neither can the others' deficiency be excused in the bad managing of the tutorship if they likewise accuse not the rest who were joined with them in the administration; for it is not only the principal tutor who may call to an account those who are suspected to have unjustly or indiscreetly ordered the affairs of their pupil, but even those who were formerly removed may also upon just occasion discharge and remove the delinquents therein. Therefore those who are obliged to serve a whole empire and kingdom, as the constables, marshals, peers and others, or those who have particular obligations to some provinces or cities, which make a part or portion of the kingdom, as dukes, marquesses, earls, sheriffs, mayors, and the rest, are bound by the duty of their place to succor the commonwealth and to free it from the burden of tyrants, according to the rank and place which they hold of the people next after the king. The first ought to deliver the whole kingdom from tyrannous oppression; the other as tutors that part of the kingdom whose protection they have undertaken; the duty of the former is to suppress the tyrant; that of the latter to drive him from their confines. Wherefore Mattathias, being a principal man in the state, when some basely connived, others perniciously consorted with Antiochus, the tyrannous oppressor of the Jewish kingdom, he courageously opposing the manifest oppression both of church and state encourages the people to the taking of arms with these words: "Let us restore the decayed estate of our people, and let us fight for our people, and for the sanctuary." Whereby it plainly appears that not for religion only but even for our country and our possessions, we may fight and take arms against a tyrant, as this Antiochus was. For the Maccabees are not by any questioned or reprehended for conquering the kingdom and expelling the tyrant, but in that they attributed to themselves the royal dignity, which only belongs by God's special appointment to the tribe of Judah.

Humane histories are frequently stored with examples of this kind. Arbactus, governor of the Medes, killed effeminate Sardanapalus, spinning amongst women and sportingly distributing all the treasures of the kingdom amongst those his loose companions. Vindex and Galba quit the party of Nero, yea, though the senate connived, and in a way supported his tyranny, and drew with them Gallia and Spain, being the provinces whereof they were governors. But amongst all, the decree of the senate of Sparta is most notable, and ought to pass as an undeniable maxim amongst all nations. The Spartans being lords of the city Byzantium sent Olearchus thither to be governor and commander for the wars, who took corn from the citizens and distributed it to his soldiers. While the families of the citizens died for hunger, Anaxilaus, a principal man of the city, disdaining that tyrannous usage, entered into treaty with Alcibiades to deliver up the town, who shortly after was received into it. Anaxilaus, being accused at Sparta for the delivery of Byzantium, pleaded his cause himself, and was there acquit by the judges, for, said they, "Wars are to be made with families, and not with nature, nothing being more repugnant to nature than that those who are bound to defend a city should be more cruel to the inhabitants than their enemies who besiege them."

This was the opinion of the Lacedemonians, certainly just rulers. Neither can he be accounted a just king, who approves not this sentence of absolution; for those who desire to govern according to the due proportion of equity and reason take into consideration as well what the law inflicts on tyrants as also, what are the proper rights and bounds, both of the patrician and plebeian orders. But we must yet proceed a little further. There is not so mean a mariner, but must be ready to prevent the shipwreck of the vessel, when either the negligence or willfulness of the pilot casts it into danger. Every magistrate is bound to relieve, and as much as in him lies, to redress the miseries of the commonwealth if he shall see the prince or the principal officers of state, his associates, by their weakness or wickedness, to hazard the ruin thereof; briefly, he must either free the whole kingdom, or at least that portion especially recommended to his care, from their imminent and encroaching tyranny. But has this duty proper relation to everyone? Shall it be permitted to Hendonius Sabinus, to Ennus Suranus, or to the fencer Spartanus; or, to be brief, to a mere private person to present the bonnet to slaves, put arms into the hands of subjects, or to join battle with the prince, although he oppress the people with tyranny? No, certainly, the commonwealth was not given in charge to particular persons, considered one by one, but on the contrary particulars even as papists are recommended to the care of the principal officers and magistrates, and therefore they are not bound to defend the commonwealth, which cannot defend themselves. God nor the people have not put the sword into the hands of particular persons; therefore, if without commandment they draw the sword, they are seditious, although the cause seem never so just. Furthermore, the prince is not established by private and particular persons, but by all in general considered in one entire body, whereupon it follows, that they are bound to attend the commandment of all, to wit, of those who are the representative body of a kingdom, or of a province, or of a city, or at the least of some one of them before they undertake anything against the prince.

For as a pupil cannot bring an action, but being avowed in the name of his tutor, although the pupil be indeed the true proprietor of the estate and the tutor only owner with reference to the charge committed unto him, so likewise the people may not enterprise actions of such nature but by the command of those into whose hands they have resigned their power and authority, whether they be ordinary magistrates, or extraordinary, created in the assembly of the estates, whom, if I may so say, for that purpose they have girded with their sword and invested with authority, both to govern and defend them, established in the same kind as the pretor at Rome, who determined all differences between masters and their servants, to the end that if any controversy happened between the king and the subjects, they should be judges and preservers of the right, lest the subjects should assume power to themselves to be judges in their own causes. And therefore if they were oppressed with tributes and unreasonable imposts; if anything were attempted contrary to covenant and oath, and no magistrate opposed those unjust proceedings, they must rest quiet, and suppose that many times the best physicians, both to prevent and cure some grievous disease, do appoint both letting blood, evacuation of humors, and lancing of the flesh, and that the affairs of this world are of that nature that with much difficulty one evil cannot be remedied without the adventuring, if not the suffering, of another, nor any good be achieved without great pains. They have the example of the people of Israel, who during the reign of Solomon refused not to pay those excessive taxes imposed on them, both for the building of the temple and fortifying of the kingdom, because by a general consent they were granted for the promulgation of the glory of God and for the ornament and defense of the public state.

They have also the example of our Lord and Savior Jesus Christ, who though he were King of Kings, notwithstanding, because he conversed in this world in another quality, to wit, of a private and particular man, paid willingly tribute. If the magistrates themselves manifestly favor the tyranny, or at the least do not formally oppose it; let private men remember the saying of Job, "For the sins of the people God permits hypocrites to reign," (34:30) whom it is impossible either to convert or subvert, if men repent not of their ways, to walk in obedience to God's commandments, so that there are no other weapons to be used but bended knees and humble hearts. Briefly, let them bear with bad princes, and pray for better, persuading themselves that an outrageous tyranny is to be supported as patiently as some exceeding damage done by the violence of tempests, or some excessive overflowing waters, or some such natural accidents unto the fruits of the earth, if they like not better to change their habitations, by retiring themselves into some other countries. So David fled into the mountains and attempted nothing against the tyrant Saul, because the people had not declared him any public magistrate of the kingdom.

Jesus Christ, whose kingdom was not of this world, fled into Egypt, and so freed himself from the paws of the tyrant. Saint Paul, teaching of the duty of particular Christian men, and not of magistrates, teaches that Nero must be obeyed. But if all the principal officers of state, or divers of them, or but one endeavor to suppress a manifest tyranny, or if a magistrate seek to free that province or portion of the kingdom from oppression which is committed to his care and custody, provided under color of freedom he bring not in a new tyranny, then must all men with joint courage and alacrity run to arms and take part with him or them, and assist with body and goods, as if God Himself from heaven had proclaimed wars and meant to join battle against tyrants, and by all ways and means endeavor to deliver their country and commonwealth from their tyrannous oppression. For as God does oftentimes chastise a people by the cruelty of tyrants, so also does He many times punish tyrants by the hands of the people, it being a most true saying, verified in all ages: "For the iniquities, violences, and wickedness of princes, kingdoms are translated from one nation to another, but tyranny was never of any durable continuance." The centurions and men at arms did freely and courageously execute the commandments of the high priest Jehoiada in suppressing the tyranny of Athaliah. In like manner all the faithful and generous Israelites took part and joined with the Maccabees, as well to re-establish the true service of God as also to free and deliver the state from the wicked and unjust oppression of Antiochus, and God blessed with happy success their just and commendable enterprise. What then? Cannot God when He pleases stir up particular and private persons to ruin a mighty and powerful tyranny? He that gives power and ability to some even out of the dust, without any title or colorable pretext of lawful authority, to rise to the height of rule and dominion, and in it tyrannize and afflict the people for their transgressions, cannot He also even from the meanest multitude raise a liberator? He who enthralled and subjected the people of Israel to Jabin, and to Eglon, did he not deliver and liberate them by the hand of Ehud, Barack and Deborah, whilst the magistrates and officers were dead in a dull and negligent ecstasy of security? What then shall hinder? You may say the same God, who in these days sends us tyrants to correct us, that he may not also extraordinarily send correctors of tyrants to deliver us? What if Ahab cut off good men, if Jezebel suborn false witnesses against Naboth, may not a Jehu be raised to exterminate the whole line of Ahab, to revenge the death of Naboth, and to cast the body of Jezebel to be torn and devoured of dogs? Certainly, as I have formerly answered, the Almighty is ever mindful of His justice, and maintains it as inviolably as His mercy.

But forasmuch as in these latter times, those miraculous testimonies by which God was wont to confirm the extraordinary vocation of those famous worthies are now wanting for the most part, let the people be advised that in seeking to cross the sea dryfoot, they take not some impostor for their guide who may lead them headlong to destruction (as we may read happened to the Jews), and that in seeking freedom from tyranny, he who was the principal instrument to disenthrall them become not himself a more insupportable tyrant than the former. Briefly, lest endeavoring to advantage the commonwealth, they introduce not a common misery upon all the undertakers participating therein with divers States of Italy, who, seeking to suppress the present evil, added an accession of greater and more intolerable servitude.

Finally, that we may come to some period of this third question, princes are chosen by God and established by the people. As all particulars considered one by one are inferior to the prince, so the whole body of the people and officers of state who represent that body are the princes' superiors. In the receiving and inauguration of a prince, there are covenants and contracts passed between him and the people, which are tacit and expressed, natural or civil, to wit, to obey him faithfully whilst he commands justly, that he serving the commonwealth, all men shall serve him, that whilst he governs according to law, all shall be sub mitted to his government, etc. The officers of the kingdom are the guardians and protectors of these covenants and contracts. He who maliciously or willfully violates these conditions is doubtless a tyrant by practice, and therefore the officers of state may judge him according to the laws. And if he support his tyranny by strong hands, their duty binds them, when by no other means it can be effected, by force of arms to suppress him.

Of these officers there are two kinds: those who have generally undertaken the protection of the kingdom, such as the constable, marshals, peers, palatines, and the rest, every one of whom, although all the rest do either connive or consort with the tyranny, are bound to oppose and repress the tyrant, and those who have undertaken the government of any province, city, or part of the kingdom, such as dukes, marquesses, earls, consuls, mayors, sheriffs, etc. They may according to right expel and drive tyranny and tyrants from their cities, confines, and governments.

But particular and private persons may not unsheathe the sword against tyrants by practice, because they were not established by particulars, but by the whole body of the people. But for tyrants who without title intrude themselves forsomuch as there is no contract or agreement between them and the people, it is indifferently permitted all to oppose and depose them, and in this rank of tyrants may those be ranged, who, abusing the weakness and sloth of a lawful prince, tyrannously insult over his subjects. Thus much for this, to which for a more full resolution may be added that which has been formerly discoursed in the second question.

THE FOURTH QUESTION

Whether neighbor princes may or are bound by law to aid the subjects
of other princes, persecuted for true religion, or oppressed by manifest
tyranny.

We have yet one other question to treat of, in the discussing whereof there is more use of an equitable judgment than of a nimble apprehension, and if charity were but in any reasonable proportion prevalent amongst the men of this age, the disputation thereof was altogether frivolous, but seeing nothing in these days is more rare, nor less esteemed than charity, we will speak somewhat of this our question. We have already sufficiently proved that all tyrants, whether those who seek to captivate the minds and souls of the people with an erroneous and superstitious opinion in matter of religion, or those who would enthrall their bodies and estates with miserable servitude and excessive impositions may justly by the people be both suppressed and expulsed? But forsomuch as tyrants are for the most part so cunning, and subjects seldom so cautelous that the disease is hardly known, or at the least not carefully observed before the remedy prove almost desperate, nor think of their own defense before they are brought to those straits that they are unable to defend themselves, but compelled to implore the assistance of others. Our demand therefore is if Christian princes lawfully may and ought to succor those subjects who are afflicted for true religion, or oppressed by unjust servitude, and whose sufferings are either for the kingdom of Christ, or for the liberty of their own state? There are many, who hoping to advance their own ends and encroach on others' rights will readily embrace the part of the afflicted, and proclaim the lawfulness of it, but the hope of gain is the certain and only aim of their purposes. And in this manner the Romans, Alexander the Great, and divers others, pretending to suppress tyrants, have oftentimes enlarged their own limits.

It is not long since we saw King Henry the Second make wars on the Emperor Charles the Fifth, under color of defending and delivering the Protestant princes. As also Henry the Eighth, king of England, was in like manner ready to assist the Germans, if the Emperor Charles should molest them. But if there be some appearance of danger, and little expectance of profit, then it is that most princes do vehemently dispute the lawfulness of the action. And as the former cover their ambition and avarice with the veil of charity and piety, so on the contrary do the others call their fear and cowardly baseness integrity and justice, although that piety (which is ever careful of another's good) have no part in the counsels of the first, nor justice (which affectionately desires the easing of a neighbor's grief) in cooling the charitable intendments of the latter. Therefore, without leaning either to the one side or the other, let us follow those rules which piety and justice trace us out in matter of religion.

First, all accord in this: that there is only one Church, of which Jesus Christ is the head, the members whereof are so united and conjoined together that if the least of them be offended or wronged, they all participate both in the harm and sorrow, as throughout Holy Scripture plainly appears; wherefore the church is compared to a body. Now, it oftentimes happens that the body is not only overthrown by a wound in the arm or thigh, but even also much endangered, yea, sometimes killed by a small hurt in the little finger. Vainly therefore does any man vaunt that this body is recommended to his care and custody if he suffer that to be dismembered and pulled in pieces which he might have preserved whole and entire. The church is compared to an edifice, on which side soever the building is undermined, it many times chances that the whole tumbles down, and on what rafter or piece of timber soever the flame takes hold, it endangers the whole house of burning; he must needs be therefore worthy of scorn who should defer to quench the fire which had caught his housetop, because he dwells most in the cellar. Would not all hold him for a madman who should neglect by countermining to frustrate a mine, because it was intended to overthrow that wall there, and not this here.

Again, the church is resembled to a ship, which, as it sails together, so does it sink together, insomuch that in a tempest those who be in the forecastle or in the keel are no more secure than those who remain at the stern or on the deck; so that the proverb commonly says, "When men run the like hazard in matter of danger, that they venture both in one bottom." This being granted questionless, whosoever has not a fellow-feeling in commiserating the trouble, danger, and distress of the church is no member of that body, nor domestic in the family of Jesus Christ, nor hath any place in the ark of the covenant of grace. He who has any sense of religion in his heart ought no more to doubt whether he be obliged to aid the afflicted members of the church than he would be assisting to himself in the like distress; for the union of the church unites us all into one body, and therefore everyone in his calling must be ready to assist the needy, and so much the more willingly by how much the Almighty has bestowed a greater portion of his blessings on us, which were not conferred that we should be made possessors of them, but that we should be dispensers thereof according to the necessity of his saints.

As this church is one, so is she recommended and given in charge to all Christian princes in general, and to every one of them in particular; forsomuch as it was dangerous to leave the care to one alone,

and the unity of it would not by any means permit that she should
be divided into pieces, and every portion assigned unto one particular, God has committed it all entire to particulars, and all the parts
of it to all in general, not only to preserve and defend it, but also
to amplify and increase it as much as might be. Insomuch that if
a prince who has undertaken the care of a portion of the church,
as that of Germany and England, and, notwithstanding, neglect and
forsake another part that is oppressed, and which he might succor, he
doubtless abandons the church, Christ having but one only spouse,
which the prince is so bound to preserve and defend that she be not
violated or corrupted in any part, if it be possible. And in the same
manner, as every private person is bound by his humble and ardent
prayers to God to desire the restoring of the church, so likewise are
the magistrates tied diligently to procure the same with the utmost
of their power and means which God has put into their hands. For
the church of Ephesus is no other than that of Colossae, but these
two are portions of the universal church, which is the kingdom of
Christ, the increase and prosperity whereof ought to be the continual
subject of all private men's prayers and desires, but it is the duty of
all kings, princes, and magistrates not only to amplify and extend the
limits and bounds of the church in all places, but only to preserve
and defend it against all men whatsoever. Wherefore there was but
one temple in Judea built by Solomon, which represented the unity
of the church, and therefore ridiculous and worthy of punishment
was that churchwarden who had care only of some small part of the
church, and suffered all the rest to be spoiled with rain and weather.
In like manner, all Christian kings, when they receive the sword on
the day of their coronation, solemnly swear to maintain the catholic
or universal church, and the ceremony then used does fully express
it, for holding the sword in their hands, they turn to the east, west,
north, and south, and brandish it, to the end that it may be known
that no part of the world is excepted, as by this ceremony they assume

the protection of the church, it must be doubtless understood of the true church, and not of the false; therefore ought they to employ the utmost of their ability to reform and wholly to restore that which they hold to be the pure and truly Christian church, to wit, ordered and governed according to the direction of the Word of God. That this was the practice of godly princes we have their examples to instruct us. In the time of Hezekiah, king of Judah, the kingdom of Israel had been a long time before in subjection to the Assyrians, to wit, ever since the king Hosea; and therefore if the church of Judah only, and not the whole universal church had been committed to the custody of Hezekiah, and if in the preservation of the church the same course were to be held, as in the dividing of lands and imposing of tributes, then questionably Hezekiah would have contained himself within his own limits, especially then when the exorbitant power of the Assyrians lorded it everywhere. Now, we read that he sent express messengers throughout Israel, to wit, to the subjects of the king of Assyria, to invite them to come to Jerusalem to celebrate the Paschal Feast, yea, and he aided the faithful Israelites of the tribes of Ephraim and Manasseh, and others, the subjects of the Assyrians, to ruin the high places which were in their quarters.

We read also that the good king Josiah expelled idolatry, not only out of his own kingdom, but also even out of the kingdom of Israel, which was then wholly in subjection to the king of Assyria, and no marvel for where the glory of God and the kingdom of Christ are in question, there no bounds or limits can confine the zeal and fervent affection of pious and godly princes. Though the opposition be great, and the power of the opposers greater, yet the more they fear God, the less they will fear men. These generous examples of divers godly princes have since been imitated by sundry Christian kings, by whose means the church (which was heretofore restrained within the narrow limits of Palestine) has since been dilated throughout the universal world. Constantine and Licinius governed the empire together, the one in the Orient, the other in the Occident. They were associates of equal power and authority. And amongst equals, as the proverb is, "There is no command."

Notwithstanding, because Licinius does everywhere banish, torment, and put to death the Christians, and amongst them divers of the nobility, and that for and under pretense of religion, Constantine makes war against him, and by force compels him to give free liberty of religion to the Christians, and because he broke his faith and relapsed into his former cruelties, he caused him to be apprehended and put to death in the city of Thessalonica. This emperor's piety was with so great an applause celebrated by the divines of those times that they suppose that saying in the prophet Isaiah to be meant by him: "Kings shall be shepherds and nursing fathers of the church" (Is. 49:23). After his death, the Roman empire was divided equally between his sons, without advantaging the one more than the other. Constans favored the orthodox Christians, Constantus, being the elder, leaned to the Arians, and for that cause banished the learned Athanasius from Alexandria, the greatest professed adversary of the Arians. Certainly if any consideration in matter of confines be absolutely requisite, it must needs be amongst brethren, and notwithstanding, Constans threatened to war on his brother if he restored not Athanasius, and would without doubt have performed it, if the other had long deferred the accomplishment of his desire. And if he proceeded so far for the restitution of one bishop, had it not been much more likely and reasonable for him to have assisted a good part of the people if they implored his aid against the tyranny of those who refused them the exercise of their religion, under the authority of their magistrates and governors? So at the persuasion of Atticus the bishop, Theodosius made war on Chosroes, king of Persia, to deliver the Christians of his kingdom from persecution, although they were but particular and private persons, which certainly those most just princes who instituted so many worthy laws and had so great and special care of justice would not have done if by that fact they had supposed anything were usurped on another man's right, or the law of nations violated. But to what end were so many expeditions undertaken by Christian princes into the Holy Land against the Saracens? Wherefore were demanded and raised so many of those Saladine tenths? To what purpose were so many confederacies made, and crusades proclaimed against the Turks, if it were not lawful for Christian princes, yea, those furthest remote, to deliver the church of God from the oppression of tyrants, and to free captive Christians from under the yoke of bondage? What were the motives that led them to those wars? What were the reasons that urged them to undergo those dangers? But only in regard of the churches' union, Christ summoned every man from all parts with a unanimous consent, to undertake the defense thereof? For all men are bound to repulse common dangers with a joint and common opposition, all which have a natural consent and relation with this we now treat of. If this were lawful for them against Muhammad, and not only lawful, but that the backward and negligent were ever made liable to all infamous contempt, and the forward and ready undertakers always recompensed with all honor able respect and reward, according to the merit of their virtues; wherefore not now against the enemy of Christ and his saints? If it be a lawful war to fight against the Greeks (that I may use that phrase) when they assail our Troy; wherefore is it unlawful to pursue and prevent that incendiary Sinon? Finally, if it have been esteemed a heroic act to deliver Christians from corporal servitude (for the Turks enforce none in point of religion), is it not a thing yet much more noble to enfranchise and set at liberty souls imprisoned in the mists of error?

These examples of so many religious princes, might well have the directive power of law. But let us hear what God Himself pronounces in many places of His Word by the mouth of His prophets against those who advance not the building up of His church, or who make no reckoning of her afflictions. The Gadites, the Reubenites, and half

the tribe of Manasseh desired of Moses that he would allot them
their portion on the other side of Jordon. Moses grants their request,
but with this proviso and condition that they should not only assist
their other brethren the Israelites to conquer the land of Canaan,
but also that they should march the first, and serve as vanguard to
the rest, because they had their portions first set them forth, and if
they fail to perform this duty, he with an anathema destines them to
destruction and compares them to those who were adjudged rebels at
Kadesh-barnea. "And what," says he, "your brethren shall fight, and
you in the mean season rest quiet at home? Nay, on the contrary, you
also shall pass Jordan, and not return into their houses, before first the
Lord have driven his enemies out from before his face, and granted
place to your brethren as well as you; then shall you be innocent before the Lord and His people Israel" (Num. 32:6, 21-22). He shows
by this that those who God first blessed with so great a benefit, if they
help not their brethren, if they make not themselves sharers in their
labors, companions in their travels, and leaders in their dangers, they
must doubtless expect a heavy punishment to fall upon them.

Likewise when under the conduct of Deborah, the Naphtalites
and Zabulonites took arms against the tyrant Jabin, and in the mean
season the Reubenites, who should have been first in the field, took
their ease and played on their pipes, whilst their flocks and herds fed
at liberty; the Gadites held themselves secured with the rampire of
the river; the Danites gloried in their command at sea; and Ashur, to
be brief, was confident in the difficult access of their mountains. The
Spirit of the Lord speaking by the prophetess, does in express terms
condemn them all: "Curse ye Meroz," said the Angel of the Lord,
"curse ye bitterly the inhabitants thereof, because they came not to
the help of the Lord, to the help of the Lord against the mighty.
But blessed above women shall Jael the wife of Heber the Kenite
be," (Judg. 5:23-24) who, though she might have alleged the alliance
which her husband had with the Canaanites did notwithstanding kill

Sisera, the general of the enemies' army. And therefore Uriah spoke religiously and like a true patriarch when he said: "The ark of the Lord, and Israel, and Judah abide in tents, and my lord Joab, and the servants of my ;ord are encamped in the open fields; shall I then go into mine house, to eat and to drink and to lie with my wife? As you livest, and as thy soul lives, I will not do this thing" (2 Sam. 11:11).

But, on the contrary, impious and wicked were the princes of Israel, who supposing themselves secured by the craggy mountains of Samaria and strong fortification of Zion took liberty to loose themselves in luxurious feasts, loose delights, drinking delicious wines, and sleeping in perfumed beds of ivory, despising in the mean season poor Joseph, to wit, the Lord's flock tormented and miserably vexed on all sides, nor have any compassion on their affliction. "The Lord God hath sworn by Himself, saith the Lord God of Hosts, I abhor the excellency of Jacob, and hate his palaces, therefore will I deliver up the city, with all that is therein, and those that wallow thus in pleasures, shall be the first that shall go into captivity" (Amos 6:8). Wickedly, therefore, did those Ephraimnes, who instead of congratulating and applauding the famous and notable victories of Gideon and Jephthah did envy and traduce them, whom notwithstanding they had forsaken in dangers.

As much may be said of the Israelites, who seeing David overcome the difficulty of his affairs and remain a peaceable king, say aloud, "We are thy flesh and thy bones." And some years after, seeing him embroiled again in troubles, cried out, "We have no part in David, neither have we inheritance in the son of Jesse" (2 Sam. 5:1; 20:1). Let us rank also with these, all those Christians in name only who will communicate at the holy table, and yet refuse to take the cup of affliction with their brethren, who look for salvation in the church and care not for the safety and preservation of the church and the members thereof, briefly, who adore one and the same God the Father, acknowledge and avow themselves of the same household of faith, and profess to be one and the same body in Jesus Christ, and notwithstanding yield no succor nor assistance to their Savior, afflicted in his members; what vengeance do you think will God inflict on such impiety? Moses compares those who abandon their brethren to the rebels of Kadesh-barnea. Now none of those by the decree of the Almighty entered into the land of Canaan. Let not those then pretend any interest in the heavenly Canaan, who will not succor Christ when He is crucified and suffering a thousand times a day in his members, and as it were, begging their alms from door to door. The Son of God with his own mouth condemns them to everlasting fire that when he was hungry gave Him no meat; when He was thirsty gave Him no drink; when He was a stranger, lodged Him not; naked, and clothed Him not; sick and in prison, and visited Him not.

And, therefore, let those expect punishments without end, who lend a deaf ear to the complaints and groans of our Savior Jesus Christ, suffering all these things daily in his members, although otherwise they may appear both to others and themselves to be jolly Christians, yet shall their condition be much more miserable than that of many infidels. For why? Were they the Jews only, and scribes and Pharisees, to speak properly, that crucified Christ? Or were they Ethnicks, Turks, or some certain pernicious sects of Christians, which crucify, torment, and persecute him in his members? No, certainly, the Jews hold Him as impostor, the Ethnicks a malefactor, the Turks an infidel, the others an heretic, insomuch as if we consider the intention of these men, as the censoring of all offenses ought to have principal relation thereunto, we cannot conclude that it is properly Christ that they persecute with such hatred, but some criminal person who in their opinion deserves this usage. But they do truly and properly persecute and crucify Christ Jesus who profess to acknowledge Him for the Messiah, God, and Redeemer of the world, and which notwithstanding fail to free Him from persecution and vexation in His members when it is in their power to do it. Briefly, he who omits to deliver his neighbor from the hands of the murderer when he sees him in evident danger of his life is questionless guilty of the murder as well as the murderer. For seeing he neglected when he had means to preserve his life, it must needs necessarily follow that he desired his death. And in all crimes the will and intendment ought principally to be regarded. But doubtless these Christian princes who do not relieve and assist the true professors who suffer for true religion are much more guilty of murder than any other, because they might deliver from danger an infinite number of people, who for want of timely succor suffer death and torments under the cruel hands of their persecutors. And to this may be added that to suffer one's brother to be murdered is a greater offence than if he were a stranger. Nay, I say further, these forsakers of their brethren in their time of danger and distress are more vile and more to be abhorred than the tyrants themselves who persecute them. For it is much more wicked and worthy of greater punishment to kill an honest man who is innocent and fearing God (as those who consent with them in the faith, must of necessity know the true professors to be), than a thief, an impostor, a magician, or a heretic, as those who persecute the true Christians do commonly believe them to be. It is a greater offence by many degrees to strive with God than man. Briefly, in one and the same action it is a much more grievous crime perfidiously to betray than ignorantly to offend. But may the same also be said of those who refuse to assist ones who are oppressed by tyranny, or defend the liberty of the commonwealth against the oppression of tyrants? For in this case the conjunction or confederacy seems not to be of so strict a condition between the one and the other; here we speak of the commonwealth diversely governed according to the customs of the countries, and particularly recommended to these here or those there, and not of the church of God, which is composed of all and recommended to all in general, and to everyone in particular.

The Jew says, our Savior Christ is not only neighbor to the Jew, but also to the Samaritan, and to every other man. But we ought to love our neighbor as ourselves, and therefore an Israelite is not only bound to deliver an Israelite from the hands of thieves, if it be in his power, but every stranger also, yea, though unknown, if he will rightly discharge his duty. Neither let him dispute whether it be lawful to defend another, who believes he may justly defend himself. For it is much more just, if we truly consider the concomitants, to deliver from danger and outrage another than one's self, seeing that what is done for pure charity is more right and allowable than that which is executed for color, or desire of revenge, or by any other transport of passion; in revenging our own wrongs we never keep a mean, whereas in other men's, though much greater, the most intemperate will easily observe moderation. Furthermore, the heathens themselves may teach us what humane society, and what the law of nature requires of us in this business; wherefore Cicero says that "nature being the common mother of mankind prescribes and ordains that every man endeavor and procure the good of another, whatsoever he be, only because he is a man; otherwise all bonds of society, yea, and mankind itself, must needs go to ruin."

And therefore, justice is built on these two bases or pillars: first, that none be wronged; secondly, that good be done to all, if it be possible. So also are there two sorts of injustice: the first, in those who offer injury to their neighbors; the second in them who when they have means to deliver the oppressed do notwithstanding suffer them to sink under the burden of their wrongs. For whosoever does wrong to another, either moved thereunto by anger or any other passion, he may in a sort be truly said to lay violent hands on his companion, but he that hath means and defends not the afflicted, or to his power wards not the blows that are struck at him is as much faulty as if he forsook his parents, or his friends, or his country in their distress. That which was done by the first may well be attributed to choler which is a short madness; the fault committed by the other discovers a bad mind and a wicked purpose, which are the perpetual tormentors and tyrants of the conscience. The fury of the first may be in some sort excused, but the malice of the second admits no color of defense. Peradventure you will say, 'I fear in aiding the one I shall do wrong to the other.' And I answer, you seek a cloak of justice wherewith to cover your base remissness. And if you lay your hand on your heart, you will presently confess that it is somewhat else, and not justice, that withholds you from performing your duty. For as the same Cicero says in another place, "Either you will not make the wrongdoer your enemy, or not take pains, or not be at so much charge or else negligence, sloth or the hindering of your own occasions, or the crossing of other purposes takes you off from the defense of those who otherwise you art bound to relieve. Now in saying you only attend your own affairs, fearing to wrong another, you fall into another kind of injustice: for you abandon human society in that you will not afford any endeavor either of mind, body, or goods for the necessary preservation thereof." Read the directions of the heathen philosophers and politicians who have written more divinely herein than many Christians in these days. From hence also proceeds that the Roman law designs punishment to that neighbor who will not deliver the slave from the outrageous fury of his master.

Amongst the Egyptians, if any man had seen another assailed and distressed by thieves and robbers, and did not according to his power presently aid him, he was adjudged worthy of death, if at the least he discovered or delivered not the delinquents into the hand of the magistrate. If he were negligent in performing this duty for the first mulct, he was to receive a certain number of blows on his body, and to fast for three days together. If the neighbor be so firmly obliged in this mutual duty of succor to his neighbor, yea, to an unknown person in case he be assailed by thieves, shall it not be lawful for a good prince to assist, not slaves to an imperious master or children against a furious father, but a kingdom against a tyrant, the commonwealth against the private spleen of one, the people (who are indeed the true owners of the state) against a ministering servant to the public. And if he carelessly or willfully omit this duty, deserves he not himself to be esteemed a tyrant and punished accordingly, as well as the other a robber who neglected to assist his neighbor in that danger? Thucydides upon this matter says that "those are not only tyrants which make other men slaves, but much more those who having means to suppress and prevent such oppression take no care to perform it," and amongst others, those who assumed the title of protectors of Greece, and defenders of the country, and yet stir not to deliver their country from oppression of strangers. And truly indeed, for a tyrant is in some sort compelled to hold a straight and tyrannous hand over those who, by violence and tyranny, he hath constrained to obey him, because, as Tiberius said, "He holds the wolf by the ears, whom he can neither hold without pain and force, nor let go without danger and death."

To the end then that he may blot out one sin with another sin, he fills up one wickedness to another, and is forced to do injuries to others, lest he should prove by remissness injurious to himself. But the prince who with a negligent and idle regard looks on the outrageousness of a tyrant and the massacre of innocents that he might have preserved, like the barbarous spectacles of the Roman swordplays is so much more guilty than the tyrant himself, by how much the cruel and homicidious directors and appointers of these bloody sports were more justly punishable by all good laws than the poor and constrained actors in those murdering tragedies. And as he questionless deserves greater punishment who out of insolent jollity murders one than he who unwillingly for fear of a further harm kills a man, if any object that is it against reason and good order to meddle in the affairs of another, I answer with the old man in Terence, "I am a man, and I believe that all duties of humanity are fit and convenient for me. If others seeking to cover their base negligence and careless unwillingness allege that bounds and jurisdictions are distinguished one from another, and that it is not lawful to thrust one's sickle into another's harvest." Neither am I also of that opinion that upon any such color or pretense it is lawful for a prince to encroach upon another's jurisdiction or right, or upon that occasion to usurp another's country, and so carry another man's corn into his barn, as divers have taken such shadows to mask their bad intentions.

I will not say that after the manner of those arbitrators whom Cicero speaks of you adjudge the things in controversy to yourself. But I require that you repress the prince who invades the kingdom of Christ, that you contain the tyrant within his own limits, that you stretch forth your hand of compassion to the people afflicted, that you raise up the commonwealth lying groveling on the ground, and that you so carry yourself in the ordering and managing of this that all men may see your principal aim and end was the public benefit of human society, and not any private profit or advantage of your own. For seeing that justice respects only the public, and that which is without, and injustice fixes a man wholly on himself, it doubtless becomes a man truly honest to dispose his actions that every private interest give place and yield to public commodity. Briefly, to epitomize what has been formerly said: if a prince outrageously overpass the bounds of piety and justice, a neighbor prince may justly and religiously leave his own country, not to invade and usurp another's, but to contain the other within the limits of justice and equity. And if he neglect or omit his duty herein, he shows himself a wicked and unworthy magistrate. If a prince tyrannize over the people, a neighbor prince ought to yield succor as freely and willingly to the people, as he would do to the prince his brother if the people mutinied against him, yea, he should so much the more readily succor the people by how much there is more just cause of pity to see many afflicted than one alone. If Porsenna brought Tarquinius Superbus back to Rome, much more justly might Constantine, requested by the senate and Roman people, expel Maxentius the tyrant from Rome. Briefly, if man become a wolf to man, who hinders that man (according to the proverb) may not be instead of God to the needy? And therefore the ancients have ranked Hercules amongst the gods, because he punished and tamed Procrustes, Busiris, and other tyrants, the plagues of mankind and monsters of the earth. So whilst the Roman empire retained her freedom, she was truly accounted the safeguard of all the world against the violence of tyrants, because the senate was the port and refuge of kings, people, and nations. In like manner Constantine, called by the Romans against Maxentius, had God Almighty for the leader of his army. And the whole church does with exceeding commendations celebrate his enterprise, although that Maxentius had the same authority in the West, as Constantine had in the East. Also Charlemagne undertook war against the Lombards, being requested to assist the nobility of Italy, although the kingdom of the Lombards had been of a long continuance, and he had no just pretense of right over them. In like manner when Charles the Bold, king of France, had tyrannously put to death the governor of the country between the rivers of Seine and Loire, with the Duke Lambert, and another nobleman called Jametius, and that other great men of the kingdom were retired unto Lewis king of Germany, brother (but by another mother) unto Charles, to request aid against him, and his mother called Judith, one of the most pernicious women in the world, Lewis gave them audience in a full assembly of the German princes, by whose joint advice it was decreed that wars should be made against Charles for the re-establishing in their goods, honors, and estates those whom he had un justly dispossessed.

Finally, as there have ever been tyrants distressed here and there, so also all histories testify that there have been neighboring princes to oppose tyranny and maintain the people in their right. The princes of these times by imitating so worthy examples should suppress the tyrants both of bodies and souls, and restrain the oppressors both of the commonwealth, and of the church of Christ; otherwise, they themselves may most deservedly be branded with that infamous title of tyrant. And to conclude this discourse in a word, piety commands that the law and church of God be maintained. Justice requires that tyrants and destroyers of the commonwealth be compelled to reason. Charity challenges the right of relieving and restoring the oppressed. Those who make no account of these things, do as much as in them lies to drive piety, justice, and charity out of this world, that they may never more be heard of.

FINIS